HISTORY OF WAKE COUNTY

History of Wake County

North Carolina

WITH SKETCHES OF THOSE WHO
HAVE MOST INFLUENCED
ITS DEVELOPMENT

By
Hope Summerell Chamberlain

PEN AND INK ILLUSTRATIONS
BY THE AUTHOR

HERITAGE BOOKS
2012

HERITAGE BOOKS
AN IMPRINT OF HERITAGE BOOKS, INC.

Books, CDs, and more—Worldwide

For our listing of thousands of titles see our website
at
www.HeritageBooks.com

A Facsimile Reprint
Published 2012 by
HERITAGE BOOKS, INC.
Publishing Division
100 Railroad Ave. #104
Westminster, Maryland 21157

Copyright © 1922 Mrs. William Johnston Andrews

Index Copyright © 1998 Heritage Books, Inc.

— Publisher's Notice —
In reprints such as this, it is often not possible to remove blemishes from the original. We feel the contents of this book warrant its reissue despite these blemishes and hope you will agree and read it with pleasure.

International Standard Book Numbers
Paperbound: 978-0-7884-1042-0
Clothbound: 978-0-7884-8091-1

Mrs. Alexander Boyd Andrews

THIS BOOK
IS DEDICATED TO THE MEMORY OF
OUR LATE BELOVED CHAIRMAN
MRS. ALEXANDER BOYD ANDREWS
(JULIA MARTHA JOHNSTON)
BY
THE WAKE COUNTY COMMITTEE OF THE
NORTH CAROLINA SOCIETY OF
COLONIAL DAMES OF AMERICA
UNDER WHOSE AUSPICES
IT IS WRITTEN AND
PRINTED

Author's Dedication

TO her just pride in her own colonial ancestry, Mrs. Alexander Boyd Andrews (Julia Martha Johnston) added a strong interest in the early history of her State. From the tradition of Mecklenburg where she was born, she came to be intensely interested in the annals of Wake, her adoptive County, and in the development of Raleigh, where she lived to be a blessing to all who knew her.

She was a patriot, as well as a Christian wife and mother; she loved the inspiration of old days, as well as the new friends she found everywhere. She was honored by being chosen as Vice-Regent from North Carolina of Mount Vernon Ladies Association. Often during her lifetime she recommended to the writer of this book the writing of a history of Wake County as a worthy work for this Committee of the North Carolina Society of Colonial Dames in America.

Thus this book becomes a memorial to her friendship and to her ideals, a sincere labor of love undertaken at her often expressed desire. It pictures the community she loved. It embodies the interests of that Committee which came into activity under her leadership. It is the fittest monument to her worth and dignity that we can raise. May she know that we remember and feel that we still love her, and approve of our dedication to her of the book she inspired.

Contents

CHAPTER I

INTRODUCTORY

Introductory Paragraph—Lawson, Explorer, 1700—Journey through the Carolinas—Visit to Falls of "News Creek"—Possibly traversed what is now Wake County—Granville Tobacco Path—Beginnings in North Carolina—Causes of great love of Liberty—Poor Government of Lords Proprietors—Locke's Fundamental Constitutions—Geographical and Topographical Conditions—Independence of Settlers—Col. Byrd's libel of Settlers—Good character of same—Growth of Settlements in North Carolina—Wake existed as parts of Johnston and Orange Counties in 1765—Tryon's Administration as Governor—Contrast between East and West of Colony—Tryon's Palace at New Berne—Grievances of Different Sections—The Regulators War—Tryon's Expedition against Regulators—Setting off of four New Counties in 1771, of which the Fourth was Wake—Tryon's Camp at Hunter's Lodge in Wake County, spring of 1771—Laying off of Rhamkatt Road—Naming of Wake County—Esther Wake, Margaret Wake, Lady Tryon—Derivation of Territory of Wake—Position in State—Soil—Products—Elevation—Climate—Streams—Raleigh Capital City and County Seat.

CHAPTER II

THE FIRST TWENTY-FIVE YEARS

Tryon's March from Wake to Alamance—The Quelling of the Regulators—Rapid Growth of Revolutionary sentiment—Thomas Jefferson's Tribute—1772, First Court held in Wake—Wake Cross Roads—Bloomsbury—Source of Name—Joel Lane's Tavern—"First Capitol"—Inscription on Tablet—Supplies furnished by Joel Lane—Inauguration of Gov. Thomas Burke—His Inaugural Address—Sketch of Burke's Life—Burke Square—Interval between Yorktown and 1789—Location of New Capital—Discussed in Intervals of Debates about the Ratification of the Federal Constitution—Account of Debate on Location of Capital—Wake County Site voted Aug, 2, 1788—Pros and Cons—Constitution Ratified 1789—Wake County Site Confirmed 1791—Willie Jones and Commissioners—Joel Lane's Tract—Laying Off of Streets—Price of Tract, etc.—Description of City Plan—Names of Streets—Park System—First Sale of City Lots—Building of State House.

CHAPTER III

Early Worthies

Number of Inhabitants of Wake County in 1800—Character of Settlers—General Mode of Life in 1800—Cotton—Transportation—Tobacco—Corn—Wheat—Live Stock—Homes—Vehicles—Horseback Riding—Amusements—Look of Country—Mode of Living of Settlers—Easy Success—Slavery—Schools—Stores and Taverns—Court Week—Religious Services—Discontent with Primitive Conditions—Prominent Citizens of Wake—John Hinton and Descendants—Theophilus Hunter and Descendants—Joel Lane and Brothers—Story of Lane's Scheming—Two Jones Families of Wake—Kinship with Allen and Willie Jones—Mingling of Blood of First Families of Wake—Fanning Jones the Tory—Dr. Calvin Jones of Wake Forest—Names of Taxpayers of Wake, 1800—Same Names to-day.

CHAPTER IV

Raleigh The Capital Village

Colonel Creecy's Description of Raleigh in 1800—Old Sassafras Tree—Governor Ashe, 1795,—First Governor Residing in Raleigh—First Governor's Mansion—Joel Lane House—Andrew Johnson House—Academy—(Old Lovejoy's) Begun 1802—Female Department 1807—Additions—Curriculum—Dr. McPheeters—Other Early Schools of Wake—John Chavis—Presentation of Globes to University of North Carolina by Matrons of Raleigh—The old "Palace" or Governor's Mansion at Foot of Fayetteville Street—Community Life of Old Raleigh—Plays—Processions—Speakings—Banquets—

CONTENTS

Census of Raleigh in March, 1807—City Government—City Watch, 1811—Art Treasure of Old State House—Story of Canova's Statue of Washington—Fourth of July Celebration, 1809—Subsequent Celebrations—First Church Edifices—List of Subjects for Further Interest in Raleigh History.

CHAPTER V

EARLY LIFE AND THOUGHT

Forgetting the New Necessary to Understanding of Old—Politics—Economics—Definition of Democracy—Federalists—Jeffersonians—Warring Ideals, French and English—Andrew Jackson—Political Change in North Carolina—State Banks—"Tippecanoe and Tyler Too"—Henry Clay—Old Whigs—Backwardness of Education—The Western Fever—Discussions of Slavery—New England's Didacticism—Internal Improvements—Canals—High Cost of Living, 1821—Stage Coach Travel—Newspapers—The Gales—Raleigh "Register"—"The Standard"—Scarcity of Books—Food in Raleigh—Furniture—Fashions—Table Ware—Housewives, Duties—The Unmanageable Young Folks of the Twenties and Thirties.

CHAPTER VI

GIANTS OF THOSE DAYS

Col. William Polk—The Old State Bank—Colonel Polk on Dueling (Alfred Jones Duel)—Colonel Polk Beats an Old Neighbor—His Dancing—His Son Leonidas—His Friend and his Cousin and his Bank Janitor—Sketch of William Boylan—Invention of Cotton Gin—Mr. Boylan's Kind Heart—His Home, Wakefield—Peter Brown—Practising Lawyer—His Return to Raleigh—Judge Seawell—Moses Mordecai—William Peck—Anecdote of State Bank Days—Young R. S. Tucker—Dr. William McPheeters—Disciplinarian—Peace Brothers—Joseph Gales and Mrs. Winifred Gales his Wife—David L. Swain—His Life—His Historical Work—Mention of Familiar Characters in the Raleigh of His Time.

CHAPTER VII
MORE BIOGRAPHIES

Notice of John Marshall—Anecdote of his Stay in Raleigh—Reference to Him from Governor Swain—Quotation by Judge Badger—Judge Gaston—Influence on Constitutional Convention of 1835—Last Religious Disability Removed by Influence of William Johnston—Gaston's Eloquence—His Piety—John Haywood, State Treasurer—Other Members of the Haywood Family—John Haywood's Friendly Ways—Popularity—Devotion to University of North Carolina—Funeral Eulogy—Judge Badger—Youthful Ability—Many Honors—Battle Family—Duncan Cameron—His Buildings—Leonidas K. Polk (Fighting Bishop)—Brigadier-General in Confederate Army—His Life, Services as Bishop and as Soldier—Brave Death.

CHAPTER VIII
IMPROVEMENTS AND PROGRESS

Stimulus of Loss—Burning of the Old State House—Destruction of Statue of Washington—Other Alarms of Fire—Miss Betsy Geddy—Controversy over New Capitol—Judge Gaston's Influence—Appropriation for New Capitol—Building Committees—Corner Stone, July 4, 1833—Same Day, Railroad Plan—Final Cost of Capitol—Its Material—Its Designers and Builders—Method of Moving Stone for Capitol—Mrs. Sarah Hawkins Polk and Her Street Cars—Spirited Raleigh Women—Poor Fire Protection—Hunter's Pond—Description from Petersburg Paper—Eagerness for Railroad in North Carolina—Capitol Finished—Railroad Comes In—Great Double Celebration—Described by Witness—Early Engines, Tracks and Cars—Time Table—Breath of Progress.

CHAPTER IX
THE MIDDLE YEARS

Rapid Progress—Establishment of Capital as Center, Political and Social—General Prosperity—Plantation Homes—Mexican War—

CONTENTS 15

Discovery of Gold in California—Effect on Men's Minds—Cheerful Temper—Great Political Campaign Waged in Wake—Educational Interest—Saint Mary's School—Wake Forest College—Free School —Growth of Population—Increase of Luxury—Of Fashion—Dress and Food—Advantage of Railroads though Despatched Without Telegraphs—Interest in Farming Methods—Culture—Reading— Discord over Slavery—Rift Growing Wider—Differing Opinions in Raleigh—Old Heads—Hot Young Hearts—The Actual Secession— After—The Surrender of the Capital as Narrated by Governor Swain—The "End of an Era."

CHAPTER X

Our Benefactors

Five Citizens—One Stranger—A Woman—John Rex the Tanner and his Bequest for a Hospital—Intention not Fully Realized and why—William Peace and Peace Institute—Dorothea Dix—Sketch of Life—Story of Founding of State Hospital for Insane—Stanhope Pullen—His Peculiarities—His Business Success—His Gifts: to City, to State, to State College for Women—John Pullen: Charitable, Consecrated—His Example—His Remarkable Funeral—R. B. Rainey—His Gift of Library to City—His Modesty—The Real Meaning of his Gift.

CHAPTER XI

Distinguished Visitors

General Lafayette—Henry Clay—President James K. Polk— President Buchanan—General Joseph Lane—Stephen A. Douglas— Mrs. Jefferson Davis—President Andrew Johnson—President Theodore Roosevelt—Woodrow Wilson, Just Before Becoming Candidate for the Presidency—Vice-President Sherman—Vice-President Marshall—State Literary and Historical Speakers—Edwin Markham— James Bryce—Henry Cabot Lodge—Jules Jusserand—Ex-President Taft—Frenchmen of the High Commission during World War— General Tyson—Dorothea Dix Several Times—Dr. Anna Howard Shaw—Miss Rankin the First Congresswoman.

CHAPTER XII

These Later Days

Life Story of a Nation—Wm. L. Saunders and Colonial Records—Self-Consciousness in History Comes Later—Early Manufacturing—Hand-loom Products—Home Dyes—Women's Handicrafts—Early Before-the-war Cotton Factories—None in Wake—Cotton Gins in Wake—Cotton-seed Oil made in Wake Before the War—Pianos made in Raleigh—Paper Mills in Wake: Joseph Gales' and Royster's—Disposal of Latter Mill—Agricultural Methods—Wartime Impetus to Manufacturing—Home Work Given Out to Country Women—Sewing—Knitting—Manufactures in Raleigh for Confederacy — Powder — Guncaps — Cartridges — Matches — Curry-combs—Metal Findings—John Brown Pikes—Wooden Shoes—Cotton Cloth Found in Devereux Mansion—Cotton Cultivation—Reconstruction Period—Priestley Mangum and Mangum Terrace—Developed More Perfectly—Walter Page—State Chronicle—Watauga Club—Agricultural and Mechanical College—Growth of Manufactures in Raleigh—Rural Free Delivery—Progress all over Wake County.

CHAPTER I

Introductory

IT is difficult to realize beginnings. Let us turn back the stream of time, let us look at our old familiar places in the light of former days. No one has stepped twice in the same river, and its onward flow changes all shores.

Who has not said to himself, as he passed along familiar streets and considered familiar landmarks,—

"*I wish I'd seen
The many towns this town has been.*"

So it is with this country we live in and possess. When we go abroad upon the hilly roads of this pleasant inland County of Wake, when we note the outlines of its ridges against the sky, and see field and forest and farm, and scenes of man's long residence, we often wish to think backward and perceive clearly these old well-known scenes with the eyes of the first European explorers as they threaded their way through forest glades, peopled at that time only by the red men.

The first historian of North Carolina, the explorer Lawson, although known to have passed through the central part of this State, cannot actually be proved to have trod the soil of Wake County. One authority on our local history thinks that he did, and indeed it seems more than possible.

Lawson made a journey through western and middle Carolina in the year seventeen hundred or thereabout. His course was a long loop coming out of South Carolina and crossing the Catawba and the "Realkin" (or Yadkin) and other streams, continuing in a northeasterly direction and then due east, until he finally reached the settlements of the North Carolina seaboard. His descriptive traveller's journal reads as fresh and as crisply interesting as if penned last year, and we get the impression of a writer alert in every sense and perception. He was a fine optimistic fellow, and though he was hired no doubt to praise the new colony, and so draw in settlers from among the readers of his account, yet no one can close his book without the feeling that he too, like many another coming to North Carolina to live, soon fell in love with the climate, and delighted to bask under the sunny sky.

Hear his account of leaving "Acconeechy Town" (which must have been near Hillsborough), and marching twenty miles eastward over "stony rough ways" till he reached "a mighty river." "This river is as large as the Realkin, the south bank having tracts of good land, the banks high, and stone quarries. We got then to the north shore, which is poor white sandy soil with scrubby oaks. We went ten miles or so, and sat down at the falls of a large creek where lay mighty rocks, the water making a strange noise as of a great many water wheels at once. This I take to be the falls of News Creek, called by the Indians We-Quo-Whom."

For a first trip through an unknown wilderness, guided only by a compass, this suggests the neighborhood, and describes the granite ridges that traverse Wake County, and produce the Falls of Neuse, where the river flows across one of these barriers.

During the next days' travel he comments on the land "abating of its height" and "mixed with pines and poor soil." This, too, makes it sound as if he perceived the swift transition which may be seen in the eastern part of Wake County from one zone to the next, from the hard-wood growth to the pine timber, and from a clay to a sandy soil.

Lawson highly praised the midland of North Carolina, between the sandy land and the mountains, and it is pleasant to read his enthusiastic account of this home of ours, and learn the impression it made on a good observer in its pristine state, and before the white man's foot had become familiar with the long trading path, which must have crossed west, near this section, but not certainly in the exact longitude of Wake County.

This trail is known to have passed Hillsborough, and to have crossed Haw River at the Haw Fields. It may well have followed the same course, as later did the Granville Tobacco Path, which certainly traversed Wake County near Raleigh.

Wake County was one of the latest of the pre-Revolutionary counties to be set off from the rest, and its boundaries were not in any sense natural boundaries, dependent upon natural barriers or the course of streams, but were run and divided for purely political reasons.

The story of the making and naming of Wake County is an interesting one, and properly to tell it requires some general account of the Colony of North Carolina and its beginnings.

The first settlement of the Carolinas was begun under the charter of a company of English noblemen, the Lords Proprietors. If these owners received their quit-rents as specified, they did not take much further interest in their plantations, nor molest the settlers; hence, the northern colony, being so neglected and more isolated, was ever the freest of all the Old Thirteen; one might even say the freest and easiest of them. Having no good harbor, and hidden behind the sand-bars from the storms of Hatteras, it enjoyed its immunity. Not being easily reached from outside, it did as its people chose with governors and edicts, dodged its taxes, harbored fugitives, and governed its own affairs quite comfortably.

The Lords Proprietors employed John Locke, the great English philosopher, to draw up a form of government for their two infant colonies, and when he did so a more unsuitable set of constitutional provisions for a thinly settled state would be hard to find.

This "Fundamental Constitution" was a confused and complicated plan full of strange titles and orders of nobility, with its "Landgraves" and its "Caciques," a plan which it would have been hard enough to follow in a populous society, with no will of its own; and which it was quite impossible to carry out in a sparsely peopled edge of the wilderness where the principal aim in life of the inhabitants was to escape all outside coercion, and to delight in space and liberty.

The confusion brought about by this famous Locke Constitution was also a cause of this glorious opportunity, eagerly grasped by the colonists, to avoid outside interference, as well as dispense with all the inconveniences of home rule and superfluous government.

Still another cause of freedom was the rapid succession of governors sent by the Lords Proprietors, some grossly incompetent, some most tyrannical, and all objectionable to the temper of the colony even when of average diligence, or because of that diligence.

The later Royal governors were on the whole better men, but the custom had gone on too long for them to subdue those who had defied so long and so successfully any other government save their own.

Again, the liberty of North Carolina was favored simply by the shape of the coast as mentioned above, indented as it is by sounds and wide tide-water rivers, intersected by great swamps, and the whole shut in from the highway of nations by shallows and sand-bars. Even neighborhoods were secluded from each other by sounds and estuaries, while the whole was protected from outside interference. The individual planter scarcely saw a dozen folk outside of his own family in a year.

This freedom of the free in North Carolina was well known, and many came to her borders to enjoy it.

The adventurous, then as now, longed for a wilderness in which to wander; the hunter wanted game, and found abundance there.

Religious sects, persecuted elsewhere, were unmolested in North Carolina; dissenters and Quakers could settle in peace. Indeed the colonists, like Sir John Falstaff, had almost forgotten what "the inside of a church was like." Those also who wanted to rub out their reckoning and begin life over again, could do so unquestioned, and those who simply wanted to make a living, could make it almost too easily for their own welfare, by half cultivating the rich bottom-lands.

At no time were there any more really criminal persons in North Carolina, in proportion to the population than there were in Virginia, although there may well have been more fugitives from the law in the strip of no-man's-land that intervened between North Carolina and Virginia before the dividing line was run and agreed upon.

One may read and smile at the witty libel of Colonel William Byrd of Westover, and note how this colony and its liberty roused the ire of the aristocratic Virginian.

He regards it as a big brother does a very impertinent smaller one who has run away and is making faces from over the fence. His chuckles are a bit spiteful as he describes the inferiority, compared with Virginia, of the "Rogues Harbor," this "Redemptioners Refuge." He waxes sarcastic over their over-primitive homes, and habits of living, choosing extreme examples; he refers to their lack of piety and churches, adverts to their love of liquor and laziness, their lack of baptism for their children and of the sanction of church ceremony for the union of the parents, and then, having had his merciless fling at them, he unwillingly acknowledges that the dividing line will have to be run fifteen miles or so north of the line that Virginia has always been claiming.

He is also forced to record that all the settlers on this strip of territory were glad to hear that they had been set off into North Carolina forever, but seems also to regret that by this means these undesirables and border ruffians were deprived of chance for future amendment.

Colonel Byrd coveted the pleasure of seeing them put to rights, although the including of them in Virginia would have seemed to spoil the high moral average of that colony according to his telling.

The fundamental nature of our population was sound and wholesome, incentive to crime was lacking; there was plenty of a rude sort, no crowding for any, and the excess of liberty was better endured there than in the west of of the eighteen-fifties, where there was gold, and the lust of it, to excite men's ambition.

Colonists were coming in great numbers by the middle of the eighteenth century. Great Indian wars were fought to a conclusion, and the west was opened up more and more, as people pushed up the great rivers. By 1765, Mecklenburg and Rowan had filled up, faster perhaps than the intervening lands. The soil grew more fertile farther west. Scotch-Irish, Moravian and Pennsylvania "Dutch", second generation pioneers, came down the Piedmont and settled the pleasant valleys.

A few years later, Salisbury and Charlotte were thriving little frontier towns and Hillsborough was almost as large as it is today.

For many years after Col. William Byrd and Edward Mosely had surveyed the dividing line, Wake County was but an undistinguished part of the middle western woods, with here and there a settler; but by 1765 it had become adjoining parts of the counties of Johnston and Orange.

It was in this same year that William Tryon came to be the new Royal Governor of North Carolina, and the colony became daily more prosperous, the west having filled up as stated, while the eastern precincts grew rich and became refined in their ideas of comfort and even luxury. Those eastern folk enjoyed agricultural abundance from the fertile soil, they plied a coastwise trade, and owned large ships trading to Bermuda and even to English seaports. Their sons were sent to be educated in England or in the northern colleges, and the leading men showed "a prevalence of excellent education" although there were no colleges and few schools worth the name in all Carolina.

The different levels of rank were as well marked in the east as in Virginia at that time, but in the west, in Carolina, as in western Virginia, the settlers were mostly Presbyterians and other dissenters, were small farmers, and did not own slaves, which were always the rule for working the broad plantations in the tide-water country.

These western folk were often pious, but if by chance some one was careless in religion he was all the more eager for liberty. Pioneers, and the sons of pioneers, some settled and some pressed on, piercing the wooded passes of the mountains and faring over into Kentucky and Tennessee. They were the second generation in the colony, Americans born, who cared nothing for the King and the "Old Home," but rejoiced to find the whole boundless continent before them. Woodsmen and explorers these, like Daniel Boone, who once settled for a little time in western North Carolina, but felt himself crowded when he could see smoke from a neighbor's fire closer than twelve miles of wilderness away.

This was the Old North State when Tryon came from England to his difficult task, that of bending the pride of the east, and subduing the independence of the west, and thus governing the heterogeneous mixture.

Tryon had many good qualifications. It is certain by evidence that he must have been a fine figure of a man; he had been a soldier; his ability was far above average; he was the possessor of fine tact, reinforced by an iron will, and a determination to govern at all costs. His first problem was the trouble about the stamp tax and he handled the news of its repeal in a masterly manner, gaining from it the full advantage in behalf of the Royal Government. Also he cunningly utilized the joy and good humor over this repeal as an opportunity for asking money to build a governor's mansion in New Berne, then the seat of government.

When we think of the dislike of all America for the word "taxes" at that date, and when we remember how unwilling our fathers then were, and their descendants still are, to spend money for governmental show and glory, Tryon is in this matter shown to be a commanding and astute manager of men. His ascendancy over the lower house of deputies, and his gaining so much of his desires from them seem little short of marvelous.

He received fifteen thousand pounds in all for building his "palace" as it began to be called, and when this was finished it was the finest building of the kind in all America. Tryon reconstructed there, as best he could, the

English ideal of polite society, and held social festivities with all dignity and due decorum; but the accomplishment of his heart's desire brought him a thriving crop of jealous comment from the wealthy planters who did not relish his sitting to receive them in his "elbow chair," nor his haughty airs in his fine house.

As to the western farmers in their log-cabins, although they were a thousand times better off than their brethren of the English countryside, and though they did not call themselves either poor or miserable, they lived hardily and had little respect for luxury, and no patience at all with what seemed to them sinful extravagance. Moreover they had a set of excellent grievances. They justly complained of the large fees for the grants and deeds to their land, extorted by the sheriffs and county clerks. The amounts of these fees are not set down as so enormous, but the King's officers were constantly accused of over-charging, and of charging twice and pocketing the difference. Also these dues must be paid in real money, of which there was very little in circulation in the Colony and which then had a much greater purchasing power than now.

Thus the men of the back country were fermenting with a spirit of obstinate opposition to constituted authority, while taxes were some years in arrears. That there was oppression and abuse seems quite certain, and also that this oppression was caused by the arbitrary and offensive behavior of the men in charge of the tax collecting.

Mingled with the ever-growing dislike of their tyranny was indignation over the expense of building that great fine palace, and added to that, an ill-defined irritation against what we might call pernicious high-brow-ism in some of the more prominent officials, especially Edmund Fanning and John Frohock.

Fanning was called Tryon's son-in-law, but authority for that is wanting. He was a graduate of Harvard College and a man tactless and arrogant, who felt and showed contempt for these frontier folk. The hatred that centered upon him cannot be accounted for in any other way. Not one voice has been raised in vindication of his doings until more than a hundred years had passed since he left North Carolina. The sting of disdain outlasts blows and injuries in the memory, and

Fanning and Frohock were so hated that they became the subjects of the first popular ballads native to North Carolina, mere prose not expressing the strong feelings of the people against them, and an ante-Revolutionary "Hymn of Hate" being necessary.

The Governor went to the western part of the State in 1770 to compose the trouble that was brewing there, which was the beginning of what is called the Regulators War, but he does not seem to have gone to the root of the matter. He simply told the people to be good, and while he had Fanning tried, allowed him to be white-washed and fined only a penny for each of the extortions as proven. Tryon could not read the signs of the times and left discontent behind him.

The Regulators were full of bitterness. It was a feeling rather than a reasoned opinion. The War of the Regulation, as it seems to our partial information, was the rising of a groundswell of Democracy.

It bore some analogy to the spirit of opposition which has sometimes possessed the mountain folk of our own and adjoining states when they thought of revenue collectors and United States revenue officers.

Mr. Frank Nash has called this "political near-sightedness" in one of his historical papers, and that expresses the condition better than any other phrase.

The backwoodsman who had traveled far and subdued a bit of the wilderness for his own, wished to be let alone in possession of what he had so hardly won. He had fought and fended for himself against crude nature and savage foes, had made his clearing and built his cabin with unaided arm. He could scarcely acknowledge the right of any one to dictate to him. Like the Irishman who said he owed nothing to posterity by reason that posterity had never been of any benefit to him, the frontiersman considered talk of this government, and of taxes owing to it, quite impertinent, while the British throne and the king over the water had no sentimental appeal to him.

His case was parallel to that of the mountaineer who finds a far-away government laying hands upon his home-made whiskey. He has made it out of his own corn, which he has often cultivated by hand on a hillside too steep to plough, and he knows that this indul-

THE OLD SASSAFRAS TREE ON THE CAPITOL SQUARE STILL ALIVE IN 1922. FROM THIS FAMOUS "DEER STAND" FORTY HEAD OF DEER WERE SHOT BY ONE HUNTER, WITHIN THE MEMORY OF THOSE ALIVE IN 1800.

gence is denied him by an outside influence and not of his own consent.

No brief is held for the moonshiner, but who can not understand the point of view of the ignorant mountaineer? Our frontiersman reasoned much in the same way, and his fees and taxes seemed enormous to him, and indeed were so, measured by his ability to pay in real money.

It was in 1771 when Tryon returned west with the eastern militia to quell this disturbance in Orange and Rowan, which grew daily more severe, and it was in that very year that Wake County came into existence. The Regulators were most active in Orange and Rowan, and the best opportunity for getting together and talking politics was then even more than it is now, court week, for that was the only time when the whole settlement turned out in a general manner.

Tryon thought it would be a good thing to divide the counties, and, so doing, divide the courts and prevent so general a free discussion. He therefore influenced his council to set off four new counties, Guilford, Chatham, Surry, and Wake, as a measure for dividing up the Regulators and silencing their general discussions. The reason given in the enactment, however, is one of distance and greater convenience in attending court. This measure was signed by Tryon in the spring of 1771.

In the record of the expedition of that same spring against the Regulators, we find Tryon camped at Hunter's Lodge, the home of Theophilus Hunter in Wake County, and said to have been about four miles from the present southern boundary of the City of Raleigh.

It is also of record that the (Ramsgate) Rhamkatt Road was laid off through the woods towards Hillsborough so as to avoid the rough hills of the Granville Tobacco Path, in hastening Tryon's military wagons.

We also note that the sign and countersign of one of those days of delay in camp at Hunter's Lodge, as they waited for recruits, were the words "Wake" and "Margaret," which suggests strongly the origin of the name of the new county. The maiden name of the Governor's lady was Margaret Wake, and the new county might well have been named for her, especially as the parish was named St. Margaret's, after her baptismal name. Esther Wake, that lovely vision whose tradition is so persistent, cannot be absolutely proved to be more than an imagination of the gallant Shocco Jones. She probably existed, but we cannot be certain of it now, and the name Wake is easily accounted for without her aid. It has very recently been noted that in January, 1771, "the Honorable Miss Wake" gave two pounds sterling for the founding of a minister and teacher for the German settlement. This shows Esther a very kindly, lovely girl.

Wake County was carved out of Orange for the most part, and included also a bit of Johnston and a little of Cumberland. In making of new counties around it later, it lost part of its first extent; but it was then, as now, the midmost county between the low country and the mountains, and is approximately central between the Virginia line and the boundary of South Carolina. It is the level where the long-leaved pines of the lower lands yield to forests of hardwood trees, and the sandy soils pass definitely into red clay. Its wonderful diversity of products is directly referable to this variety of soil, and the two

A perfectly preserved example of the simpler farm-home of the early days of Wake County standing near Apex. This house has a brick built into the upper part of its chimney bearing the date "1775" and its woodwork corresponds with that date

edges of the county, eastern and western, are as distinct as though a hundred miles separated their boundaries.

The first ridges of any regularity of extent which cross the State from north to south, the first ripples of those folds which rise into the great Blue Ridge, cross Wake County. Almost all varieties of soil not strictly alluvial are found in some part or another of Wake, and indeed there is often the greatest difference in the constitution of the soil of different sides of the same field. The climate also is about the medium between the damp of the east and the keen light air of the mountain section. Neuse River and its tributary creeks drain and water it well. Raleigh, the Capital of the State for more than a hundred years, occupies almost a central point in the County, and has been until now the only large town of the County.

CHAPTER II

The First Twenty-five Years

FROM Theophilus Hunter's in Wake County, Tryon marched direct to the Battle of Alamance, where the Regulators were beaten, their army dispersed, and six of their ringleaders quickly hung for treason.

So thorough were his methods that all active hostility was then over. But although their armed resistance was quelled, the "embattled farmers" of North Carolina went to their homes with that bewildered feeling of frustration and utter disaster that left them neither self-confidence for future attempt, nor expectation of any redress for their crying grievances. The public debt which Tryon incurred in this expedition, added to the arrears bequeathed to him by his predecessors, was never paid; nor would it have been easy to collect from a people more and more indignant, more and more weaned from its allegiance to Great Britain.

The New England Colonies treading the self-same path, sent emissaries to North Carolina to test the temper of its people, and never did sentiments of liberty meet greater sympathy, or aspirations for independent existence more favor. The people of North Carolina were ripe for revolution. Wrote Thomas Jefferson at this time, "There is no doubtfulness in North Carolina, no state is more fixed or forward."

In this year of transition and bitter brooding was held the first court in the new County of Wake, and we know who located the county seat at Wake Cross Roads, and named it Bloomsbury, which name had never appeared before in this place. This was also done by the Tryons, and the name of Bloomsbury must be referred to them, as being the name of a new suburb of London, just then being "developed" as we say of real estate ventures.

Russell, Earl of Bedford, was building this part of London on a portion of his ancestral acres, and he is said also to have been responsible in some way for Tryon's appointment as Colonial Governor. Russell Square, which is so often mentioned in Thackeray's novel, *Vanity Fair*, as the home of the heroine, was in Bloomsbury, and is the actual name of a street there. This name must have meant something of home and London to the Tryons, as is shown by their giving it to this corner of the wilderness. Here is a likely connection.

On the contrary, we cannot see any reason why Joel Lane, born on this side of the ocean, and busy, enterprising wild-westerner as one might call him, should fancy and insist upon the name of Bloomsbury more than any other English name. He probably was glad to adopt a name which the Governor suggested for his tavern. This western Bloomsbury was a mere stopping place beside the Hillsborough Road, and the first court was held in the residence or tavern of this Joel Lane, already one of Wake County's most prominent citizens. There was a jail of logs, and our first sheriff was named Michael Rogers. Theophilus Hunter was a justice, and so were Joel Lane and several other of the men whose names occur first on the records. The old court corresponded to the English Quarter Sessions and has been long superseded by the later constitutional arrangements of North Carolina.

There still stands, in the western part of Raleigh, a rather small house with a very steep gambrel roof, in the style of architecture common at the beginning of the nineteenth century and before, called the Dutch Colonial. This house used to face Boylan Avenue, standing a little back from the street, but was moved a few years ago, and now faces the south side of Hargett Street near the State Prison.

The exact year of its erection is not known, but its architecture is of the same order as that of the house at Yorktown, Virginia, where Cornwallis surrendered to General Washington.

It also resembles in angle of roof the little "Andrew Johnson Birthplace" which stands restored in Pullen Park, and another historic house at Edenton, where was held the Edenton Tea Party. The peculiar, quite steep slant of the roof over the second story has been disused in more modern houses, and serves as a means of dating the erection.

This house on Hargett Street was once known as the "First Capitol," and was built by and belonged to Joel Lane. It may well have been new at the time we are describing It was considered a very fine house in its day, and is called the "best house within a hundred miles."

Probably those same old walls that we all have seen were those that sheltered the first county court, and there Tryon certainly stopped on his return from the military expedition against the Regulators. It could scarcely have been built during the troubled times of the Revolution, and could well have been in existence in the year 1772, as it is of record that it was in 1781.

On the street corner near to its first situation a boulder has been placed, and a bronze tablet let into its side bears the following inscription, placed there by the Daughters of the Revolution, Bloomsbury Chapter, in the year 1911.

ON AND AROUND THIS SPOT STOOD THE OLD TOWN OF BLOOMSBURY OR WAKE COUNTY COURT HOUSE

WHICH WAS ERECTED AND MADE THE COUNTY SEAT WHEN WAKE COUNTY WAS ESTABLISHED IN 1771. THIS PLACE WAS THE RENDEZVOUS OF A PART OF TRYON'S ARMY WHEN HE MARCHED AGAINST THE REGULATORS IN 1771

HERE MET THE REVOLUTIONARY ASSEMBLY IN 1781, AND TO THIS VICINITY WAS REMOVED THE STATE SEAT OF GOVERNMENT WHEN THE CAPITAL CITY OF RALEIGH WAS INCORPORATED IN 1782.

Tryon and his lady left North Carolina in 1771 for New York State, he to become Governor there, and North Carolina never saw either of them again. It is said that they were glad to go in spite of having to leave the fine house they had built in New Berne, because the climate had not suited their health nor the spirit of the colony their minds. When the Revolution came on, Tryon County in the west was promptly divided into Lincoln and Rutherford and the Governor's name thus expunged from our County roll; but the name of Wake spoke neither of defeat nor oppression.

Gallant North Carolina would not flout the Governor's lady, and Wake remained the name of a county, and shall ever remain so called, whether named originally for that lovely shadow, Esther Wake, or for her fair sister, Lady Tryon.

The Revolution called on every man to rally to his colors. Tories were plentiful and active in North Carolina. The former Regulators strangely did not come to the help of the Congress very freely, but seem to have been cowed or disgusted with fighting, and stood aloof, not enlisting on either side. The Wake County militia volunteered, and from the sparse population many men went to war. We will not follow these, but, remaining at home, will mention a few points of distinctly Wake County history.

We have already described Joel Lane's home, called the "First Capitol," and it was there that the General Assembly of North Carolina met in the month of June, 1781. The Capital of the State had been a movable institution for some time previous, being appointed to meet at first one town and then another, according to the necessities of a country at war. Records were thus many a time lost, and it is wonderful that we possess intact as many as we do, considering the difficulty of keeping up with such a shifting capital. As a measure of safety perhaps, Wake County was made the choice of this troubled year, almost the lowest ebb of the American cause. At this meeting Joel Lane was voted the sum of fifteen thousand pounds for the lodging and food of the General Assembly and the pasturage for their horses. His guests must have been as addicted to fried chicken as the preachers are accused of being, for the next item of allowance is one to Vincent Vass, "for candles and fowls" eighteen hundred pounds.

These are not such great sums as they sound, for the colonial currency of paper money became extremely depreciated as the Revolution went on, just as the Confederate paper money did years afterward in the war between the States; and by this time it was worth no more of its face value than is indicated in the saying, "not worth a Continental."

A good horse would bring twelve hundred pounds in the money of that year, and we may estimate by this that the members of Assembly probably had no more chicken than they needed.

Another event of this Wake County session of the Assembly, much more noteworthy, was the inauguration of a Governor of North Carolina, which was, prophetically, held for the first time in Wake County inside the area of the future capital of the State, while as yet it was not. The war-time Governor was Thomas Burke of Orange County, and the announcement of his election to the Governor's office was formally conveyed to him at the tavern at Wake Court House, at the beginning of this first Assembly there convened.

His speech of acceptance, his inaugural, on that occasion, refers to the difficulty of his task, and especially mentions the activities of the Tories, the condition of the colony almost verging on civil war, and the lack of proper support from the people to the State Government.

Burke was a well educated man, and had assisted in drafting the State Constitution adopted for North Carolina at the time of the Declaration of Independence at Philadelphia. He was an Irishman from Galway and a Catholic, but although he lived in a far more intolerant age than ours, the fact of his religious belief was never mentioned against him. According to English law, which was the foundation of the law of the colonies, none but Protestants could hold office, and of Protestants only Church of England men. In the colonies, however, this rule had already been ignored before the Revolution, and dissenters had become governors of North Carolina under the old government. No one now asked anything of Governor Burke save as to his patriotism.

Burke lived near Hillsborough, and was further distinguished as being the very first of the poets in this State, except only those nameless ballad-makers among the Regulators. His further adventures are of interest.

In September of that same year, 1781, the Tories under David Fanning (a name of bad odor, but no relation that we know to that Edmund first mentioned) came up in force from the southern counties, with the publicly avowed aim of capturing the Governor of North Carolina.

They raided Hillsborough, then called the capital. David Fanning was a native of Wake County, and a Tory bushwhacker; he knew the lay of the land. His band surprised the defenceless village of Hillsborough one night, and while Burke and his friends seem to have been expecting them, and to have resisted with spirit, the Tories were too many for them, and Burke was captured and carried to Wilmington, then in British possession. Thence he was taken to Sullivans, and later to James

Island off the coast of South Carolina. Being held imprisoned by the expanse of ocean about this island, he was set free on parole there. He felt most unsafe, his life being threatened by a lawless band of Tories living on the island, and was forced to hide from place to place.

Being, as he said, in such danger of his life, he broke his parole and escaped, returning to North Carolina. Arrived there he immediately resumed his office as Governor. The leaders of the army and of civil affairs do not seem to have known quite what to do about his actions. A man at liberty on parole, even though supposedly confined by the limits of an island and who had broken that parole to escape, appeared to them not quite an honorable man, much less a hero, and as such, unworthy to hold the office highest in the state. Burke, however, felt himself justified, and showed no scruples on the subject.

On April the twenty-second, 1782, Burke having at last found that the sentiment of the people and the Assembly was against him, asked of his own accord to resign, and the Assembly consented with great alacrity.

The name of Alexander Martin was proposed to supersede Burke, while a vote of thanks and recognition of his service was passed to permit his retiring with full dignity.

Burke died during the next year at Hillsborough, his home. Burke County, North Carolina, was named for him, not for the other greater Irishman, Edmund Burke, who gave expression in England to the creed of American freedom. Burke Square, where our Governor's mansion stands today, was also named for him and no other, and had he not fallen upon such trying times and puzzling circumstances, his name might shine undimmed by even a bit of poor judgment.

It has always appeared to the careless reader of history that the interval between the surrender of Cornwallis at Yorktown and the association of this state with the rest of the Union was an eneventful and negligible time, because it was not signalized by dramatic events, as was the period of Revolutionary struggle just past.

We are required to count those seven or eight years long years, and to conceive the various perplexities they brought, in order to see what a risk and what an experiment this government of ours was considered at first, and how many new questions pressed for solution upon the leaders everywhere, especially upon the members of the Constitutional Convention of Philadelphia.

It was clear enough that the Articles of Confederation which had been strong enough to unite the colonies against a common foe during the Revolution, could not sufficiently hold together the differing interests of the different states, during their period of recovery from the damage of the war. It was to meet those new internal dangers that the Constitution of the United States was framed.

Our fathers builded better than they knew. When drawn up, the Constitution was submitted to each of the states for its approval by vote of its representatives. Nine states, by approving the articles, would make the Constitution valid for all. North Carolina summoned her Constitutional Convention to consider the new Constitution and recommend any amendments considered necessary to its adoption by herself.

This was done, and those amendments which were recommended stand mostly embodied in the United States Constitution today, all four being concerned with personal and states rights, which were not considered sufficiently guarded in the first draft, to satisfy our individualistic ideas in old North Carolina.

At the second Constitutional Convention in Fayetteville, amendments had been adopted by the Philadelphia convention, many states had already ratified, and North Carolina was content to fall into the procession. This assembly voted to ratify the Constitution at once, this being in November, 1789, and North Carolina being next to the last state to enter the Union. This is all general history, but what makes it necessary to review it here is the fact that the location of the City of Raleigh, and its choice as our permanent capital, was mixed and sandwiched in with the grave and searching consideration of the Articles of Constitution. This was because the task was set for this first convention, not only of criticising and later ratifying the Constitution of the United States, but also of choosing a proper seat of government or state capital for North Carolina.

"The first Constitutional Convention of North Carolina was held at Hillsborough on the twenty-fifth of July, in the year of our Lord 1788, in the thirteenth year of the independence of the United Colonies of America, in pursuance of the resolution of the last General Assembly, for the purposes of deliberating and determining on a proper form of Federal Government; and for fixing the unalterable seat of government for this State."

Thus runs the opening phrase of the report of this convention. A full delegation was present, five from each county represented the best minds and most patriotic hearts of the land. The delegation from Wake consisted of Joel Lane, Thomas Hines, Brittain Saunders, James Hinton and Nathaniel Jones. Governor Samuel Johnson presided as Governor of the Colony. The debate of the delegates shows a good deal of opposition to ratification on the part of the extreme Jeffersonians, led by Willie Jones of Halifax. The second part of their task, that of fixing an "unalterable seat of government" was attended with many jealousies and bickerings. This is a matter of tradition as well as of record, and even mixed into the conventional phrases we may today trace bitter rivalry between the west and the east, between one town and the other. Tradition has it that Willie Jones was a master at log-rolling and took a hand for his friends in this free-for-all contest.

The first motion making this business the order of the day was made by Mr. Rutherford of Rowan, seconded by Mr. Steele, his colleague, also of Rowan. "Resolved, that this Convention tomorrow at four o'clock in the afternoon fix on a proper place for the seat of government."

This resolution was passed but protested against by Mr. Blount of Beaufort County. Next day, accordingly, a committee was selected to choose places for the Convention to vote upon in turn "Exact spot not to be fixed, but that it be left to the discretion of the Assembly to ascertain the exact spot; provided it be within ten miles of the point or place determined by this Convention."

This defined indefiniteness is accounted for by considering that the provision was made in order to prevent the speculation in land that could suddenly be brought to pass if the spot should be more definitely located. Besides, we may consider that conditions as to water

Wakefield, the residence of Joel Lane. Built before 1770. Removed after 1900 to its present location. This picture shows it on its old site on Boylan Avenue.

and water courses, and levels and slopes were not entirely known, and room for adjustment would be afforded in a twenty-mile diameter.

The following places were voted on by the Convention. Smithfield, Tarborough, Fayetteville, The Fork of Haw and Deep Rivers, Mr. Isaac Hunter's Plantation in Wake County (placed in nomination by Mr. Iredell of Chowan), New Berne, Hillsborough.

On ballot Mr. Isaac Hunter's plantation in Wake County was fixed on for the future location of the Capital in its immediate neighborhood. This vote was taken on August second, 1788.

Willie Jones of Halifax (being, as a living man an astute politician, and none the less still to be reverenced as one of our constructive statesmen so long after his death), seems to have moved on the stormy waters at this juncture, and to have shaped things to his mind.

Just why he wished to locate the Capital in Wake, and why he moved in such mysterious ways to that end, the terse record does not show; but tradition insists that he did a good deal of the dealing, and as we are too far down the river of time to review his conclusions, we will just be satisfied with the result, and be glad he made so good a selection, using his so great influence to bring it about. From out the past comes a whisper about the recipe which he used for apple toddy, and about supper at Joel Lane's tavern. Surely they slander the city's founders who repeat this old story! Scarcely was the vote counted when Mr. Barry Grove of Fayetteville entered a protest on the following grounds: "First, because the situation chosen is unconnected with commerce and can never rise above the degree of a village. The same mistake has been made in the selection of Williamsburgh and of Annapolis, and the result is seen there. Secondly, because Fayetteville would have a great effect upon commerce, being a thriving town at the head of navigation."

This protest was signed with one hundred nineteen names, and would indicate that the opposing factions, though strong, did not get together quite early enough to thwart Mr. Jones or accomplish their own wish.

The west wanted Fayetteville or Hillsborough; the eastern section was divided, each delegate wanting the chief town of most convenient location in his own immediate neighborhood; and rather than vote for a rival town would vote for a western place, by this means restraining the rival from profiting.

Thus the vote being so close and so doubtful, a committee was appointed to report later upon this matter, when the constitutional convention should meet at Fayetteville the next year.

Accordingly, in the autumn of 1789, the Convention ratified the United States Constitution with far less wordy war than they had expended upon the question of a site for the capital the year before. The committee which was to report upon the matter of the seat of government was not ready at that time and made its recommendations two years later, by which time all the tumult and shouting had finally died, and the matter was settled once for all in favor of the Wake County site.

Fayetteville still felt aggrieved and said so, and her indignation was reasonable enough, but such compromises are very often made.

Perhaps we should be justified in raising a statue to the memory of that great Jeffer-

The Old State House, destroyed by fire in 1831.
(From a painting by Jacob Marling, in the Hall of History.)

THE FIRST TWENTY-FIVE YEARS 61

sonian, Willie Jones, as the real founder of Raleigh, for to his interest the actual parceling out seems due. Nine commissioners were given the task of laying off ground for the new city, and selecting for that purpose among the various tracts offered.

The names of the commissioners were James Martin, Hargett, Dawson, McDowell, Blount, Harrington, Bloodworth, Person, and Willie Jones, and while all did not actually ride over the various lands, all have their names perpetuated in the names of streets of Raleigh.

Joel Lane's tract was chosen, and a thousand acres of land bought from him. Part of this land was originally Mr. Lane's, but part belonged to Theophilus Hunter of Hunter's Lodge, was sold by him to Mr. Lane a short time before, and was bargained for by the commissioners as part of the Lane tract. The original Lane land ended at Morgan Street and all south of that line was Mr. Hunter's. This purchase is the greater part of the land where the city of Raleigh now stands. At that time it was covered with primeval forest, and some old oaks are still standing which must have shaded the surveyors who run off the streets and carved our city squares out of the virgin wilderness.

On Friday March thirtieth, 1792, the final decision was made, and boundaries located. The price paid to Lane for the whole tract of land was two thousand seven hundred fifty dollars, which does not sound like a fancy price for a selected square mile of land.

William Christmas was the surveyor, and was paid one hundred ten dollars for his work after he had finished laying out substantially the same streets and squares that we tread in our daily walk at this date.

The Capitol Square is the largest, in the center of the city. Four other squares were left open to form parks, and named Caswell, Nash, Burke, after the three Governors of those names, while the fourth was called Moore, after the first Attorney General, who afterwards became Associate Justice of the United States Supreme Court. Streets were named after Stephen Cabarrus, William Lenoir, William R. Davie, and Joel Lane, besides the commissioners as named above. The streets which ended at Capitol Square, and those bounding it were named after the leading towns of the state at that time—Hillsborough, Fayetteville, Halifax, New Berne, Salisbury, Edenton, Wilmington, except Morgan, which is named for what was then a judicial district.

One wonders why there was not a Charlotte Street, according to the plan. Fayetteville Street was at one time afterwards known as LaFayette Street, but the change has not persisted.

Raleigh was born a city. No wandering pre-historic cows laid out her streets and marked her thoroughfares, as was the case with older settlements. Her name was ready for her two hundred years before, and was bestowed at the suggestion of Governor Alexander Martin, and her charter had been granted in 1587 when Sir Walter Raleigh attempted a permanent settlement on Roanoke Island. This historic name was inevitably hers. It was the only name that could have been given with propriety to a capital of North Carolina. The infant city stood clothed in forest, with streets blazed among the trees. The four avenues which ended at the Capitol Square,

"The Old Mordecai Place" in Raleigh. The back of this house is very ancient. The front elevation is also old, but not earlier than the Joel Lane and Haywood houses.

then named Union Square, were much broader than the rest, and the only criticism we can offer to the worthy committee who laid out our town is that they might have made all the streets as wide, seeing that land was cheap and paving unknown. It is not wonderful that no vision of automobile traffic and street railway system visited their minds, but they did show a great foresight in giving us a park system, foresight which their descendants have done their best to nullify, for in our great economy we have built up two of these four squares which were left open for us and for our children, and we shall always have to keep repenting our short-sightedness.

After the City of Raleigh was thus laid out and named, lots were sold to pay for the building of a State House. The commission who attended to this were R. Bennehan, John Macon (brother of Nathaniel Macon), Robert Goodloe, Nathaniel Bryan, and Theophilus of Hunter's Lodge.

The architect of the first Capitol was Rhody Atkins, whose name was not again mentioned. The floor plan was quite similar in form to the present building, but much smaller, plainer, and built of rough brick. The brick was burned for the building on lots 138 and 154 of the original survey.

The old Capitol turned its back on Hillsborough street. It faced the east according to the custom of many another public building erected at that epoch. It cost the State of North Carolina twenty thousand dollars when complete, and was enough enclosed in 1794 so that the Legislature met that year for the first time in the "New State House" in the City of Raleigh.

The members of assembly boarded in the neighboring farm houses and at Joel Lane's tavern, and rode in to their work each day on horse-back. Scarcely anyone lived as yet in the limit of the city proper. The State House stood in solitude, surrounded by its mighty oaks for the most part of the first decade. Raleigh was like any other town created by legislative act, crude and struggling at first.

Washington was the same kind of capital on a far larger scale; but both have long outgrown their awkward age.

CHAPTER III

Early Worthies

LIFE just after the Revolution was a much simpler manner of existence than it is now, especially as regards worldly possessions. In 1800, there were but ten thousand people in all Wake County, and many of these were negro slaves, although not so many servants were thought necessary in proportion to the white folk as it was customary to hold in the eastern counties where the lowland climate made agricultural labor difficult for Caucasians.

The names of the most prominent citizens of Wake County in the last days of the eighteenth century and the beginning of the nineteenth were the same surnames which usually occur in the meager records of assemblies and conventions of the early pre-revolutionary time. These fathers as members and as delegates showed much practical sense and wonderful comprehension of public questions; they were also possessors of many a fertile acre of uncleared forest; their spirit was that of the eager pioneer whose prospects were fair before him, but whose present possessions did not hamper him enough to become a daily care.

The importance of the cotton crop was not yet apparent. Whitney's cotton gin was not yet invented, and the four or five pounds of cotton which one person could laboriously seed in a day, would not afford so much lint as was needed for home consumption. Those were the days of the small cotton patch planted to supply the spinning wheel and loom, and each child and every servant of the home must seed his shoe full of cotton, each winter evening before going to bed, as his regular task.

Tobacco was the crop which brought in money or exchange. It exhausted the new land very quickly, and was hard to transport over the rough roads of the settlements, but it was nevertheless an all-important means of paying for any imported goods, and a regular medium of exchange in North Carolina as formerly also in Virginia. Much of what we read in that time before railroads, about the prime importance of locating the towns upon rivers, was considered true, because it was an easy means of readily transporting tobacco to a good market.

Wheat was raised in sufficiency and corn in great abundance. The response of the virgin soil was wonderful and the climate was as fine then as now. The farmer whose family did not live in plenty was a man who would not take the trouble to raise the food he could easily cultivate. Great herds of pigs roamed the woods and lived on acorns and nuts, half wild, only coming at intervals to be fed a little corn when they heard the shrill halloo of the slave whose duty it was to look after them. Cattle, too, roamed the woods and were only a little more tame, coming up to be milked as they chose.

All the house work halted when the bell-cow's jangling bell was heard in the clearing, and the women quickly went to milk the herd, whatever the hour of day.

Houses were small and simple, log-cabins well or ill-built, single or double, and all chairs and small furnishings were home-made. Only now and then was there some prized chest or high-boy which had been brought from the last station of the pioneer family, or even from old England direct.

Vehicles were confined to wagons and gigs, and a family carriage was as much of a rarity in the early years of the nineteenth century as an automobile was in the latest ones. Ladies rode pillion, behind their men or their servants, or singly if attended. Everyone expected to ride horseback as well for a long journey as for a short one.

Hunting and fishing were the chief sports, but racing was universal in a country so dependent as this upon good and spirited horses; but there seems to have been no regular race-track in Wake County at this early date. Shooting matches for beef were held and conducted much like the famous match described in "Georgia Scenes." Cock-fighting was a common sport, the taste for which came from England with the Colonists. Wherever a few people could gather from the thinly settled neighborhoods, they enjoyed dancing and fiddling, and such amusements were participated in by young and old alike.

As to the look of the country, we know that the forest and the old field bore such a great proportion to the cultivated cleared land that farms were far apart. Only here and there did a home stand out against a wooded slope, here and there a slim spiral of smoke betray a human habitation behind the trees, or a cleared field show the work of the settler. Roads wound for miles through unbroken woodland, and the cultivated fields seemed but patches.

This life was not a poor one, although it was extremely simple. It was independent, it was self-respecting. It was full of rude plenty and wholesome work, of hope and expectation. A poor man could make a start and be sure of getting a living while paying for his land. He would raise a little stock and a pair of colts. His log-cabin cost him little beside the time he took to build it, and he need never go without his simple food and clothing and his necessities provided that he was a good shot, and that he and his wife were industrious. Slavery lightened the tasks of those who could get far enough ahead of the world to afford the purchase of a servant or two. With all its faults it was a life which had an upward slope to it, and a hopefulness for the future which kept it stimulating.

There were practically no schools in Wake County for the first years of its existence, and after the Capitol stood lonely on its hill in the midst of the new City of Raleigh. At various cross-roads were taverns where men met. Court week called them to Raleigh sometimes, and occasionally a preacher passed through and services were held; but the children were mostly left to home instruction and to the educating influence of practical experience and the many absorbing interests of their backwoods homes and their free life in the open.

The leading spirits were not satisfied with this state of things, however. There were a few men of education and refinement in Wake County from the first, and all these were prominent in the State history and politics of their day.

The first name that appears in the Colonial Records showing active service and prominence in the new county of Wake was John Hinton, who lived on Neuse River near Milburnie. He owned enormous tracts of land along the Neuse under grant from Lord Carteret, and when in course of time Wake County was divided from Johnston County, his residence fell within its boundaries. His residence was called Clay-Hill-on-the-Neuse.

He had moved from Chowan (the part now Gates County), about the middle of the eighteenth century, and his father's name before him was John Hinton. He married Grizelle Kimbrough, and had eight or nine children who reached maturity. John Hinton was Major in the provincial troops of Johnston County, and was thus called to aid Governor Tryon in the expedition against the Regulators. He was made Colonel of the Wake County troops in 1771, and was in command of his men at the Battle of Alamance. Governor Caswell mentions that he was an eyewitness of Colonel Hinton's gallant behavior on this occasion.

Colonel Hinton lived near the home where his descendants still live. He was a prominent man in the Revolutionary struggle, offering himself at once to the American cause. He served in the first Provincial Congress at New Berne, was appointed Colonel of North Carolina troops, was present at the Battle of Moore's Creek Bridge, was a member of the Council of Safety for Wake County, and acted always the part of the brave patriotic gentleman he was.

He died in 1784, leaving several minor children, and besides his own personal service two of his sons were in the Revolutionary Army. John Hinton the third, his eldest, was commissioned as Major, and James Hinton was Colonel of a troop of horse.

James Hinton above, married Delilah Hunter, daughter of Theophilus Hunter of Hunter's Lodge. Two of the daughters of Colonel Hinton successively became wives of Joel Lane, one dying quite young. Thus the Hinton family was connected with those few other families which seem to have shared with them the first possession of the broad acres of pristine Wake County wilderness, and the moulding of the little community by their service and examples.

The descendants of these people are here with us today, and their blood runs in the veins of many who never have traced out their pedigree sufficiently to be proud as they justly may be of their fine old Revolutionary ancestry.

Hinton James, the first student that registered at the newly opened University of North Carolina, and another Hinton who graduated with him in the first class, were both grandsons of Colonel John Hinton of Wake. Judge

Henry Seawell married a daughter of John Hinton, son of Colonel John Hinton, Second, the first of the name to settle in Wake.

Theophilus Hunter of Hunter's Lodge appears first as the host of Governor Tryon, and his plantation was the headquarters of the expedition of 1771 during its halt of several days in Wake County. It was at his plantation that the recruiting was done for Tyron's Army, which is recorded as having been so slow and so unsatisfactory, the smaller farmers holding sympathy with the Regulators.

Theophilus Hunter the elder was the presiding justice of the first county court ever held in Wake County, and when the first court house was moved from Joel Lane's tavern, Wake Cross Roads, or Bloomsbury, by whichever name one chooses to call the place, to its present site on Fayetteville street, Theophilus Hunter and James Bloodworth each conveyed half an acre adjoining to the then justices of Wake County and their successors in office forever, for the nominal sum of five shillings; and upon this piece of ground the new court house was then built, and successive buildings have occupied the same lot.

This property has become so extremely valuable, that some time since there was an idea of its being sold, and some land purchased which might not be quite so valuable, although quite as convenient for the purpose. Upon looking into the old deeds it was found that to use this ground for any other purpose beside the designated one of locating a court house upon it, would forfeit it to the heirs of the givers.

Besides giving a lot for the court house, Theophilus Hunter also gave a lot for a masonic lodge. This lies on Morgan and Dawson streets, Raleigh.

Theophilus Hunter, besides being a justice and a Mason, was a Major in Colonel John Hinton's Wake County Regiment during the Revolution, afterwards Lieutenant Colonel, County Surveyor, and a member of Assembly several times. He left a family of sons and daughters who married into the Hinton and the Lane families and thus drew closer the family kinship and solidarity of the first families of Wake County. He lived at Spring Hill, south-west of where the State Hospital for the insane now is. The old mansion still remains on the eminence near this old site, rebuilt into part of the State Hospital, the outdoor colonies for epileptics being located near the spot. His son, Theophilus, Jr., inherited Spring Hill and rebuilt it. The landed possessions of these men were extensive, their land reaching almost to Cary in a southwesterly direction. Isaac Hunter, brother of Theophilus, Sr., owned that plantation within ten miles of which Raleigh should be located, and his place was to the north of the city. Descendants of both these men are among our citizens today, notably the brother last mentioned has many although none of his own name, the inheritance of blood having gone through the female lines.

Theophilus Hunter Hill, a poet, and one of our few singers, was a grandson of the Hunters of Spring Hill. At the very beginning of the war of 1861, he published a slender volume of lyrics and sonnets, and after the war another volume.

He had genuine feeling and power of expressing it, and several sonnets of his are exquisite, but for the most part his poetry seems an echo of what had pleased him in his wide reading of other men's writings. It is not racy of the soil, and his images are academic, but he shows nevertheless a vein of real poetic inspiration which time and the times did not develop in the least, the stress and strain of the war extinguishing poetic fancy, and leisure and stimulation both being lacking to the perfecting of his gift.

Joel Lane with his two brothers, Joseph and Jesse, who were not so well known as himself, also had a great deal to do with the early shaping of Wake County.

O. W. Holmes, in a humorous poem, describing the portrait of his great-grandmother when a young girl, plays with the idea of what might have been the result if that dainty maiden had chosen a different suitor, when she answered 'Yes' to her life-mate, and thus had thrown the stream of inheritance into a different channel. He quaintly asks,

"Should I be I, or would it be
One tenth another and nine tenths me?"

In similar fashion we may well wonder what would have been the differing traits in the likeness of the good people of Wake County if busy Joel Lane and his brothers had chosen another path through the wilderness, and those dozen others whose blood lives today in many a citizen, "solid and stirring in flesh and bone," had settled beside some other river.

Joel Lane, who helped lay out the boundaries of Wake and the streets of our city, land-owner, mine host of Bloomsbury Tavern, Colonel in his father-in-law's Wake County regiment, purveyor of supplies for the Revolutionary Army, Associate Justice at Wake County Court in 1771 and for many years thereafter, delegate to the Provincial Congress at New Berne, member of the Council of Safety for this district, State Senator for Wake for thirteen sessions of the Assembly, planter, speculator in real estate, did not let all these activities exhaust his abundant energy. It would not take many citizens such as he to make a town progressive and lively even in these strenuous days.

He seems vividly alive to the mind as he is exhumed from old records dusty with the passing of a century. His nature must have been kindly, and his disposition sunny, to

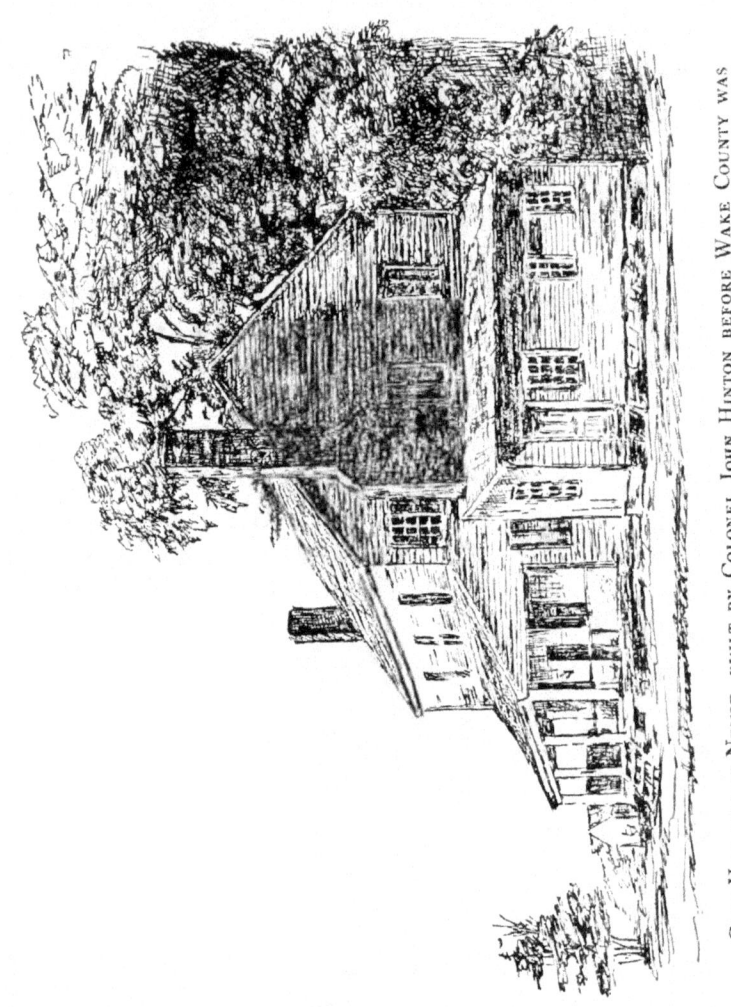

Clay-Hill-on-the-Neuse, built by Colonel John Hinton before Wake County was set off, and the oldest house left standing today in Wake County

have made him so universally liked. His house we have all seen, and it looks small and plain enough to us; but it represented to the people of that time what Governor Swain calls "a rare specimen of architectural elegance." Joel lived in this well-known house of his in the sense of the often quoted words, "by the side of the road, to be a friend to man;" and in turning the pages of the records, those dry bones of history, we may note and admire the human attraction of the way people gravitated to his tavern for their various meetings. It must have been pleasant staying there, which speaks well for the character of mine host, although we must wonder where in the world he took care of so many legislators. Probably, after the good old custom, log-cabin "offices" or bachelor quarters flanked the central dwelling, and in these he put his gentlemen guests. Very few ladies went traveling in those days.

Joel Lane's two wives were both daughters of Colonel John Hinton, who lived near Neuse River, and they brought him a fine colonial family of six sons and six daughters. Joel always adhered to the Church of England.

The Lanes are descended from the Ralph Lane who first came to North Carolina with the unlucky colony in 1585, and then sailed back to England in 1586, being succeeded as Governor by John White who left a handful of lonely white settlers to lose themselves in the western wilds, and become one of the mysteries of fate to this day. The spirit of the old seafaring Lanes still drove him "Westward Ho" and Ralph returned after a time. Joel and his brothers were already the third generation of Lanes born in the American Colonies. Their descendants have half populated Wake County, and have sent good citizens to Alabama, to Tennessee, to Missouri, and to far away Oregon. Among them are numbered governors, judges, a general and a vice-presidential candidate, a cabinet officer, too,—all men in the public eye, while they have also furnished scores more of excellent folk of the race who, while not so conspicuous, have built up their own communities more quietly for generations.

Joel Lane has been criticised because his sale of land for the location of Raleigh seemed a bit of sharp practice at the expense of his father-in-law, Colonel John Hinton, who also had a square mile of land for sale; it is even hinted that people generally resented this and that it cost him his seat in the Assembly for the next term thereafter. These hundred-year-old rumors are hard to verify. Let us use our imagination in all charity, and think that he knew what a very pleasant home for the State's central government would result from his success.

He offered a square mile of land near Cary as a free gift, should it be decided to place the University of North Carolina there, and one wonders why this offer was not accepted. He was one of the first Board of Trustees of the new institution, and had two grandsons in the first graduating class. His friendliness brought him friends and his friends showed him favor, which was surely his desert. He died in 1795, and his grave was plowed over and obliterated by Mr. Peter Brown, a Scotchman and a lawyer, who acquired his home by purchase, a few years after Joel Lane was dead and gone. Mr Brown in his turn sold the place to the first Mr. William Boylan, early in the last century.

"Spring Hill," later home of Colonel Theophilus Hunter. He built the smaller house in the rear. His son Theophilus added the larger mansion in front.

A tablet to the memory of Joel Lane was recently placed in the Municipal Building of Raleigh by the Daughters of the Revolution. One of Joel Lane's brothers was the progenitor of the Lanes of Alabama and the other was the ancestor of those who sought the far west and became prominent there. Carolina Lane, his sister, was mother of David L. Swain, and lived her whole life in Buncombe County near Asheville.

Another pre-revolutionary family connection was that of the Jones' of Wake County. There seem to have been two distinct families at first, no known kin, and living in different parts of the county, both well known for intelligence and property acquired. Besides this fact, two men, one from each family, bore the unusual name of Nathaniel, and of these, one named his eldest son after himself; hence it requires more than an ordinary genealogist to reconstruct their respective family trees, and this all the more because they complicated and confounded things still worse by intermarrying once or twice a few years later, after the second generation had grown up.

The first Jones to reach Wake County was Francis or Frank Jones, who settled on Crabtree Creek near Morrisville. His deed from Lord Carteret bears the date 1749. He bought more land adjoining in 1761. His two sons, Nathaniel First of Crabtree, and Tignall, or Tingall, were often mentioned in County and State records. This Frank is said to have been a brother of the father of Willie Jones and General Allen Jones of Halifax. If this is so then these two distinguished men were own cousins to the Jones family of Crabtree. This was the General Allen Jones who gave his name to a penniless adventurer, John Paul, whom he had befriended, and who asked at parting, if the Jones surname might be added to his own, promising that if permitted so to add it he would also add fame to it some day. This he did most wonderfully, as all those who have thrilled at the story of John Paul Jones and the *Bon Homme Richard* can testify.

Perhaps this cousinship gives one of the reasons for the residence in Raleigh of Willie Jones, during the last years of his life. This great Jeffersonian bought the plantation where Saint Augustine's School for the colored race now stands, and in the spot where the garden of the school now is, he lies buried in an unmarked grave. Though an agnostic, Willie Jones also gave the land for a Methodist Church, where Edenton Street now stands, according to several authorities. He died about the first of the new century.

To return to the Jones family of Crabtree. Nathaniel the second of Crabtree, married a daughter of John Kimbrough. His name appears as member of Assembly from Wake in both House and Senate before 1801. His son, Kimbrough Jones, was a member of the Constitutional Assembly of 1835, and he has many descendants. John Kimbrough, the father-in-law, does not come so often into the records, being perhaps a man busy with his plantation alone, but he owned more slaves in 1800 than anyone else, except James Hinton and Tignall Jones.

To continue the Wake County Joneses: Nathaniel Jones of White Plains near Cary, came also from Eastern North Carolina. His ancestors are buried in old Bath Church, and he came to what is now Wake County in 1750. Nathaniel of White Plains was, as I have said, supposed to be no known kin to Nathaniel of

The Home of General Calvin Jones at Wake Forest. (Taken from a print)

Crabtree. His father was of Welsh blood, and bore the Welsh-given name of Evan. Nathaniel of White Plains married into the Lane family, and his daughter Sarah married her cousin, John Lane, son of Joel. They went west, and their son, born in Tennessee was named Joel Hinton Lane. Of course there were many others of this family, but I give this instance to show the strong mixture of pioneering blood which must have been the very elixir of life in that "Winning of the West" which became the task of their generation.

Finding the records of all these intermarriages of the Jones families, and adding to them the more recent connections of these with the Cadwallader Joneses of Hillsborough and noting the constant recurrence of familiar Wake County surnames and Welsh patronymics among the lists of children, one realizes how hopeless and how useless it is to try and untangle the skein of these families.

There stands, however, a desolate house with vacant windows and grinning rafters, a high four-square old house, dating from the Revolutionary time, but which has been deserted many years. It stands near the town of Cary to the west, and its story was told to me by an old lady who remembers traditions, and who was somewhat kin to the former owner, Fanning Jones, but who was not proud of the relationship.

Whether his name means a relationship of connection with the notorious Tory leader who stole the Governor, or whether it is merely a coincidence, no one can now declare, but he is said for some vague reason to have forfeited the regard of his patriotic relatives, and to have been driven from the neighborhood for that reason. The Old Tory, they called him.

Doctor Calvin Jones on whose plantation Wake Forest College was located was a later comer into the county from the North. He sold his place to the Trustees of the Baptist School for two thousand dollars, which was considered cheap even in those days, for six hundred acres, equipped with buildings. Doctor Jones sold this at sacrifice in order to move to Tennessee, and mentioning him here, too early as to time, but in order to distinguish him, we will add that he was a distinguished physician and that he had a fine war record for the war of 1812, having raised a Wake County troop of horse for the army.

Besides these people whom I have called out of the past, and not speaking of others perhaps as prominent and as useful, we must recall the forbears of many of our citizens of today, living in simple homes, leaving no record of wealth, save the ownership of the acres which they had won from the wilderness and tilled for themselves with their own hands. A random reading over of the tax payers whose names were enrolled in Wake County in the year 1800, such a list as appears in the State records, yields many of the most respected and honored names of today—many names seen on church rolls, painted on signboards, and on office windows, names which have been marked by flags on Memorial days in the cemetery and which only yesterday have been engrossed and hung in the vestibules of churches, names marked on service flags with blue stars, and some after awhile with golden ones.

The father and son, and the mother and daughter also, these are those who have redeemed the wilderness, peopled the solitude, fought in Revolutionary ranks in blue and buff, and many years later have worn Confederate grey. They have done the hardest work of the new land, and the harder of the land grown populous, they whose descendants have fought and fallen on the fields of France so lately, these plain people of whom the world is made, and for whom it was made, and who shall carry the work on by their descendants into many a tomorrow.

CHAPTER IV
Raleigh the Capital Village

COLONEL CREECY in his "*Grandfathers Tales*" describes the look of the City of Raleigh in the year 1800 and for some years thereafter. He says, "It was a town of magnificent distances, of unsightly bramble bush, and briers, of hills and morasses, of grand old oaks and few inhabitants, and an *onwelcome* look to newcomers."

At that time the first State House stood solitary on the Capitol Square and near it was the famous sassafras tree, which had long marked a wonderful deer stand whence forty deer had been shot by one hunter's rifle, within the memory of those then alive.

Governor Ashe was the first governor to make Raleigh his permanent residence, and he came to town in 1795, while the other State officers also found it necessary to "go out there in the woods to live, and help with the government." The first Governor's mansion was a plain frame building on Fayetteville Street about where the Raleigh Banking and Trust

Company's building now stands. By 1800 there were two hotels. The first one, Casso's, still stands on the corner of Morgan and Fayetteville Streets opposite the State Library Building, is especially in excellent repair, and were the fire escapes and such modern additions taken away, would remain much as it used to be when the stages rolled to the door. The second was called the Eagle, which was demolished in April 1922, to erect a new State Department Building

One handsome residence had been built in Raleigh which is standing today, and has been kept in repair, remarkable beside for the fact that it is still inhabited by the representatives of the family that built it. There is no other residence so old in town or county today, beside "the old Burke Haywood Mansion" on New Berne Avenue, built in the year 1794, of which we may confidently say, as it is today so it was almost identically, more than a hundred years ago.

There were homes and stores along Fayetteville Street—small frame buildings long since burned or demolished; the Joel Lane house stood near where it now stands, but facing

South Boylan Avenue; the Mordecai place was partly built; the old Andrew Johnson birthplace, judging by the style of architecture was then in existence, but tradition says that it stood near the plot where Tucker's Store was built immediately after the war of '61. From thence it was moved at that time to Cabarrus Street, where it remained until 1900, when the local Committee of the Colonial Dames of America had it taken down board by board, and reconstructed, exactly, in Pullen Park, where it is now preserved as a relic.

There was no church edifice in Raleigh in 1800, although services were frequently held by the several denominations in the State House.

There were no common schools in all North Carolina, and but few pay schools. In the year 1801, Raleigh asks for state aid in establishing an academy, and also petitions for the use of Burke Square (where the Governor's mansion now stands) for its site.

In 1802 the plans for the building were made, fifty feet long and twenty-four feet wide, with fireplaces at each end both above and below stairs. My authority says brick, but the expression is so vague, perhaps it merely means that the great chimneys were brick, and not the whole building. In 1807 a building for a "Female Department" was added. This was one-story and smaller. The school was supported partly by tuition fees and partly by private subscriptions to bonds or shares. All the State officers' names of that day and those of nearly all the townsfolk besides were to be found on its lists.

In 1813 another building was built, the two larger buildings were insured for two thousand dollars each, while the Female Department carried two hundred and fifty dollars. Tuition was nine dollars a year and the rolls of honor and other school notices published in the newspapers of the time show that many of the pupils were from other places and boarded in town. By the year 1817 one hundred eighty pupils were in attendance. The first teacher engaged was named German Guthrie, the second Maurin Delaigny, a French refugee, a Huguenot minister, who afterwards went to Charleston and became pastor of the old Huguenot Church there.

In 1810 came Doctor William Mc.Pheeters who was principal of the Academy for many years, and also "Town Pastor," preaching on Sundays in the State House and holding Sunday School there. His salary was eight hundred dollars a year. His school throve, and soon he required assistants in his work. The course included Latin, Greek, Mathematics, English, Geography, and Bible, and his scholars ranged from beginners in reading to those who would go next year to the University. No Latin or Greek was taught to the girls, but a course in "alphabetical samplers" and wool work took the place of the classics for them.

There were other schools in the county, and some were very efficient, especially the one at Wake Forest which afterwards was enlarged into Wake Forest College. Besides this one the schools were more or less intermittent, being private enterprises.

One of the Raleigh schools deserves mention for the oddity of its human interest.

John Chavis was a negro slave, who was sent by his master to Princeton College, and educated as a Presbyterian minister. This was done as an experiment on the part of his owner, to see what could be done with a negro's mind, as I have been told by the older people. John had a good understanding and a docile disposition. When, after his years of training, he was returned home an educated man of some refinement, it became a problem to know what should be done with him. He was an ordained Presbyterian minister; he could not be sent back to the negro quarters; nor could he be recognized as a social equal. He was set free, and he was permitted to use his learning in instruction of youth. He taught in Raleigh in 1808, instructing poor white children in the day, and colored youth at night. He afterwards kept school in other parts of the State, and prepared many prominent young men for college with great success. I have heard stories told of how on occasion, he might be at some white planter's house at meal time, and how the plantation darkies would come to peer into the windows of the dining room at the Great House, to see "dat nigger John Chavis" sitting over at his side table by himself, but nevertheless, actually eating his dinner in the same room with Old Massa and Old Miss. That was the way the problem was finally solved as to the exact social position of John Chavis.

Before leaving the subject of educational uplift in Raleigh, let me chronicle the doings of the leading matrons of the town in the year 1802. They then presented a pair of globes to the scientific equipment of the infant University at Chapel Hill. The names of of the donors were as follows: S. W. Potter, Eliza Haywood, Sarah Polk, Anna White, Martha McKethan, Margaret Casso, Eliza Williams, Nancy Bond, Hannah Paddison, Susannah Parish, Ann O'Brien, E. H. P. Smith, Nancy Haywood, Priscilla Shaw, Rebecca Williams, Winifred Mears. This is probably a list of all the ladies who made up Raleigh society at that date, and shows these good women ready and efficient in helping worthy causes as their descendants and successors have ever since striven to do.

A brick mansion was built about 1813, just opposite the foot of Fayetteville Street, and outside the then city limits. It stood where the Centennial School stands now. It was a large simple building, with no architectural pretensions, and was paid for out of the proceeds of lots in the City of Raleigh sold for the

This is part of the Old Raleigh Academy, where Dr. Wm. McPheeters once taught. Latterly called Lovejoy's School. (From a photograph taken just before it was torn down to make way for the Governor's Mansion)

purpose, being those which remained in the possession of the State up to that time. These lots did not bring as great a sum as was hoped, by reason of the hard times prevailing after the War of 1812. This mansion, always known as the Governor's Palace, is the one occupied by all Governors in succession from 1813 up to the War of '61, and Governor Swain adds in dignified phrase, "The Executive office was then, as now, contiguous to the Palatial Residence."

The little town of those early days was in feeling and deportment always the capital. We read of plays staged, of processions and festivities, of speakings patriotic, and speakings commemorative, and of regular religious services all held in the State House, which was then even more than since, the center, and one might say, almost the circumference as well of all Raleigh's social life.

Banquets in celebration of the national anniversaries, not on a strictly temperance plan, were held at the hotels and occasionally out of doors at the mineral spring near the Palace. These inns were good ones, because of the many gentlemen who had to be entertained at certain seasons of the year, whose number would have strained the small private accommodations of the place.

On great occasions tables were even set in the rotunda of the State House and toasts were drunk on patriotic excuse to "every State in the Union," and the fact that there were not nearly so many states then as there are now is the reason the devoted banqueters lived through the test.

The census of Raleigh on March 23, 1807, as published in the Raleigh *Minerva*, gives white males 255, white females 178, freedmen 33, slaves 270, total 786, families 85. Governor Swain also gives these figures. The apparent overplus of bachelors in Raleigh at that time is noticeable, there being seventy-five or more unattached men. This must mean that the State officials were written down as residents whether they had brought their families to live in the town or not.

Raleigh had a commission form of government in those early days, similiar to that of the City of Washington now, being governed by the direct authority of the Assembly. It also had a town watch which patroled the unlighted streets at night, and kept the slaves from wandering abroad. There were twenty classes who took turns. This same plan was universally followed in the larger towns throughout the South.

The names of the Captains of the Watch for the year 1811 were Henry Potter, Isaac Lane, William Scott, William Boylan, Joseph Gales, Thomas Emond, Southey Bond, John Wyatt, Joseph Peace, Samuel Goodwin, Beverly Daniel, William Peck, Willis Rogers, Sherwood Haywood, William Jones, John Raboteau, James Coman, Benjamin King, Robert Cannon, and Jacob Johnson. This last name was that of the father of the President Andrew Johnson.

We may gather a good many good home-sounding names from this collection, although they made their rounds more than a century ago, and all sleep dreamless sleep tonight while others are watching.

The war of 1812 having been fought to a glorious finish, and the Algerian pirates having been smoked out by Admiral Decatur, the America name became more respected and the flag more distinguished abroad, while

England was no longer a present fear to our nation as it had been since the Revolution. Our nation began to feel its full destiny as favored of heaven. We might say of ourselves in our growing vigor and importance as a nation,

"No-pent up Utica contracts our powers."

This happy time when there was little political or sectional bitterness or other jealousy was called the "era of good feeling." The Revolution was receding into the historic past, and its heroes loomed grander, and less distinct, as their doings passed out of ordinary day-light into the shadowed aisles of history. The great consequences of these deeds were more and more realized, as time unfolded its changes.

There was in this village capital of North Carolina ninety years ago one treasure which we would give a great deal to possess, and to be able to point to, in our Capitol of today. I refer to the famous statue of General George Washington, first President of the United States, which was made by Canova.

In November, 1815, the Assembly of North Carolina passed a bill authorizing the purchase of a statue of the great and good George Washington, to be placed in the State House, and setting no limit to the cost of such a work of art.

The people of North Carolina had a right to be proud of their appreciative admiration for Washington, and the delight they took to honor his memory honored themselves also.

It was a charming bit of extravagance, and not like the strange freaks of spending that attack stingy folk once in a lifetime, but the result of pure idealism,—the fact of a heroic figure impressing the imagination of a whole people, so that they were intent upon pouring out the precious ointment of their hearts to his memory.

The motion for obtaining this statue was first made in the House by Thomas Spencer of Hyde County. His descendants, if there are any, should be proud of their ancestor for this deed.

Governor Miller, the then executive, consulted Senator Turner and Senator Macon in Washington, and they in turn consulted Thomas Jefferson in his retirement at Monticello. It was decided that only the best was worthy of the greatest American and of the State of North Carolina, and so the Ambassador to Italy from the Federal Government was commissioned to bespeak a portrait statue of Washington from Canova. Canova was the greatest sculptor then alive, unless Thorvaldsen of Sweden be named as his equal.

When asked to undertake the commission from the State of North Carolina, he put aside many orders to accept it, on account, he said, of his extreme admiration for the genius of the great Washington, and for his noble deeds. The statue was executed in Carrara marble, white as snow. The figure was larger than life. When finished, it was brought to Boston on a United States war vessel commanded by Captain Bainbridge, a hero of the Pirates' War. From Boston it was transshipped to Wilmington on a coastwise vessel, and it arrived there in 1821. From Wilmington to Fayetteville, it was floated up the Cape Fear River.

William Nichols, father of Captain John Nichols, who lived at that time in Raleigh and was in charge of the improvement of the Capitol and of other building for the State at the

University, was put in charge also of this task. It was for him to contrive means of transporting those heavy marbles over the long rough miles between Fayetteville and Raleigh. That he did so successfully is another tribute to his practical ability. On the ninth of November, 1821, word came that the wagons bearing the precious blocks of marble were near, the entire population of Raleigh, Governor, State officials, and many citizens of other parts of the State as well, went out in procession along the Fayetteville road to meet the train of wagons, and bring them into the city with a band and speeches and rejoicings.

Colonel William Polk pronounced the oration. He was living in Raleigh as president of the First State Bank. He was a Revolutionary veteran, and had been a friend of Washington, and personally associated with Lafayette. He was father of Leonidas K. Polk, afterwards the "fighting bishop," and was cousin to President Polk.

His speech on this occasion was solemn and stately, and he rhetorically declared that it was but meet and fitting that the degenerate

The old Governor's Palace at foot of Fayetteville Street. Built about 1813, and last used by Governor Vance. Torn down and replaced by a school building. (From a print)

Italian nation should add the refinement of art to the rough but vigorous patriotism of the American Republic, now far more than Italy the inheritor of the spirit of ancient Rome. This is but the impression of a long past perusal and not a direct quotation.

The statue, when unpacked and set in position in the rotunda of the old State House by Mr. Nichols seemed, to the critical eyes of many who had seen Washington in the flesh, a good likeness as regarded the countenance. Our good people, not aware of artistic license, were, however, quite struck dumb by the fact that the Father of His Country was dressed in a Roman Consul's costume, with toga, bare legs, and sandaled feet. This made them wonder and stare.

Washington was represented seated, with a tablet on one knee, on which he was writing his farewell address with a stylus. The attitude was balanced and graceful, the face calm and grave. The figure sat upon a Roman curule chair, and this rested upon a pedestal, which was sculptured on all four sides with bas-reliefs, showing notable scenes in the public service of Washington.

The sculpture exhibited Canova at his best, in which the stone was made to take a finish that seemed almost as smooth to the touch as it appeared soft to the eye, so perfect was the working, so delicate the surface. The great Lafayette, when he came to Raleigh in 1825, vouched for the correctness of the likeness as he surveyed it. The statue was the pride of the people of North Carolina. Judge Gaston said of them, "Limited in their means, plain in their habits, economical in their expenditures, on this subject they indulged in generous munificence." It was suggested by some practical soul, that a statue so valuable being now placed in a building not fireproof, should be mounted on low wheels to permit of its being moved in case of fire, but this suggestion was laughed to scorn. It is hard to guess now, in this age of wheels, why it was thought to be so undignified, so very funny to mount the statue in this way, for the sake of its safety. Had this been done, we might well possess it today, for it might have been easily saved from destruction.

Only for about ten years did the State own this art treasure, for all of that period easily the finest example of high art in all America. The mother of the writer saw this statue in in 1830, and though but a child at the time, she ever remembered it with a vivid impression and has described it minutely to her children. Mrs. A. B. Andrews had a most exact picture of it, from an Italian source, entirely authentic. Also there is an engraving with Lafayette and Miss Haywood standing looking at it. In the year 1910 owing to the indefatigable effort of the Hall of History, a cast had been made from the model, and sent as a gift from the King of Italy. The lost treasure in its beauty is a vivid personal regret. The poor mutilated fragments of the trunk and pedestal which occupy one corner of the Hall of History speak eloquently of its fate but tell little of its glory.

Canova the great Italian sculptor, was at the height of his fame and reputation when he made the statue. He was called the true inheritor of the classical tradition. He always used the mannerisms of the antique statues he studied, as well as followed the real beauty of their conception. He is now somewhat superseded in artistic esteem being considered too artificial, too smooth, although many lovely works of his are still cherished.

The old Raleigh Community revelled in processions as well as banquets. Fourth of July was always a fair chance to enjoy a parade. Hear the account of a celebration of the ever-glorious Fourth which took place in the year 1809. "At twelve o'clock, a procession of citizens and strangers, with Captain Calvin Jones' troop of cavalry, formed at the State House during the ringing of the State House, Court House, and Town bells, and the firing of the cannon. Being seated in the Commons Chamber, an ode in honor of this day, composed for the occasion, was sung by a choir of seventy voices. Reverend Mr. Turner (the principal of the Academy) delivered an oration. At three o'clock the company sat down to an excellent dinner prepared by Mr. Casso (keeper of the Hotel), which was served in the State House. Colonel Polk and Mr. Potter presided and toasts were drunk to the Governor, Mr. Nash, to the Supreme Court of North Carolina, to Literature, Science and Art, to the University of North North Carolina, to the Constitution of North Carolina, and to 'The social circles of life.' "

It was the custom of Doctor William McPheeters a few years later to hold a sunrise service on the Fourth of July, and to preach a patriotic sermon, which was always well attended, and very impressive. Reverend Drury Lacy kept up this custom of the town afterward. Following this came an oration by some good speaker, the reading of the Declaration of Independence, a procession of all the Sunday School children down Fayetteville Street to the "Palatial Residence" and then half way back again to the sound of the bells of the town. Dispersing there, everybody attended a picnic and barbecue in Parrish's Grove, at the corner of Davie and Blount Streets, and opportunity was given for all the courting and matchmaking that the daylight would hold. At nightfall, the streets being unlighted, and the ways long, the population called it a day and went home.

In calling up pictures of the town that then was, I have failed to mention the beginnings of the various religious denominations, although by the time the State House was burned there were three churches in Raleigh. The Presbyterians had a congregation organized in 1806, but as Dr. McPheeters was the only regular pastor in town for a long time, services were held in the State House, and they did not build until 1817. The early Methodists led the way, and built a little church where Edenton Street Church now stands, and by the next year the Baptists also had a small church building finished.

In 1820 the Episcopal Church was organised, and by 1826 they had begun a church on the present site of Christ Church. Later we find Duncan Cameron chairman of the building committee which made Christ Church of today, one of our really lovely buildings.

There had also been in Raleigh for some time a sort of crazy parson, a Mr. Clendenning, who had a pet heresy and preached it on Sundays. On weekdays he sold goods over his counter, and had plenty of ability and common sense to make money in his mercantile business. He seems to have been a sort of town joke.

Having tried in the foregoing chapters to bring back the idea of the old times as they really were, we must next try to recall some of the great men, and draw their characters, some of those who moved about the streets of our old capital, and made impression on our institutions. Many were not natives of Raleigh, and yet were nevertheless a part of its life, and a boast, to be pointed out to strangers sojourning in our gates as they moved on our common ways. We must revive the shock of the burning of the State House. We must learn something of the struggle and final successful anchoring of the State capital here in Raleigh, for when the State House was burned, of course the other claimants revived their claims.

Beside this we must bring out those old tales which make former days alive, and restore to us the atmosphere so long dispersed, together with the likeness of those who were a part of the passing panorama.

We must go down the roaring forties, and make ourselves by all means catch the feeling that pervaded the world before the War of '61, and thereby moulded history; not forgetting that very often feeling is far stronger than policy.

The history of a people is the history of the the minds in it, as worked upon by the soul-currents of the age, which pass no one knows how, like the wind that bloweth where it listeth.

CHAPTER V

Early Life and Thought

E must now forget the path we have traveled to our present day conception of things, throw away all those beliefs and ideas which have crystallized in our lifetimes, and think away modern conveniences and conditions and a collection of uncertainties and questions that exist no more. If there is "no new thing under the sun," yet old ideas are seen in very novel combinations as time goes on.

Look at the politics of those elder folk, and by politics I mean the prevailing conceptions of right and expediency in governmental policies, rather than party or partizanship; what real correspondences do they show to the political questions of today?

Look at their economics. With the whole continent beyond him to choose a residence from, what need was there for the old North Carolina farmer to intensify, to economize, or to farm constructively?

He need not suffer in an environment that did not suit him, he could go west, he could take up new land to replace the fields he had cleared and exhausted. Nothing hindered the restlessness of the frontiersman.

Fiscal and money problems were not well understood even in Europe of this time. The question of the best way to guard the money capital needed for all this expansion, had been settled neither in theory nor experience by any financier. While the time of the formation of the constitutions of the United States and of the several States had revealed a farsighted statesmanship which it would be hard to match today, yet all was a great experiment. No one knew how well it was going to work, and only time could reveal its flaws. We disagree honestly today on many matters, but we have settled most of the questions which exercised our grandfathers.

A caustic wit has called Democracy "the rule of the planless man," but it was not plans which were lacking in that seething time when remnants of old English monarchical conservatism and the newest and wildest of French Revolutionary theories were striving to combine into something different from either.

"The broadening of human thought is ever a slow and a complex process." Our old time Federalist did not correspond to any of the political partizanships of today and his party passed away with the echoes of the War of 1812. In his time he represented the conservative element, but no special privilege save that of education, and the able leadership it gave.

The leaders of the Jeffersonian popular party distrusted the educated few, because as they said, they were "too far from the people to understand their ways." The old Federalists had for their successors the Whigs, while the Jeffersonian, afterwards called the Republican, and lastly the Democratic party, represented the ideals of liberty as advocated in the French Revolution.

England of just after the Revolution was a very conservative, hard England, but in America no such degeneration of the democratic gospel took place; the rise of the plain people, the opportunity of the common man to become uncommon, was the opportunity of all in America.

Andrew Jackson, "Old Hickory" as he was called, born in North Carolina, called to office from Tennessee, well expressed his party as President and as popular hero.

In politics North Carolina was naturally democratic, but the majority of her leading intellects happened to be Whigs, and many of her best prophets were without honor in their own country.

The money organization of the United States was the field of many experiments. Jackson was of the opinion that money matters were best left to each sovereign state, and so he abolished the Bank of the United States, distributing its surplus pro rata among the states. This institution was doubtless a very imperfect one, but had afforded a central stable valuation of credit. Now there were as many values and measures as there were states, all the way from the "wild cat" banks of the west, to the conservative institutions of New England. Following the changeless law of finance, all the better money was hoarded and the worse put in circulation. Each state had a State Bank which bore the same relation to its finances as did the United States bank to the United States funds, and there came to be a strange mixture of money, with so many banks issuing notes which were more or less good at a shorter or longer distance from the banks of their origin.

The habit of mind about money is a great part of the mental furniture of a man, because it disposes him to honest dealing and honest success, or disposes him to the taking of too heavy risks.

The early years of the nineteenth century were far too much given to the sporting conception of things, and loose ideas about money have given more trouble to our people than has any fallacy which has survived into the present.

When, after the unlucky Democratic administration of Van Buren, the scale tipped toward the Whigs, every one but the inside bosses thought of Henry Clay as the Whig choice for President.

It is not clear just how his nomination was defeated, but defeated it was, and Harrison won it, Tyler, who succeeded him, being Vice-President, after Harrison had only been a few weeks in office, and had died. Tyler proved not to be a Whig at all, but merely an admirer of the man Clay.

So far as we can see, he was nominated Vice-President because of his gift of ready tears over the defeat of his friend. Next term, 1844, Clay lost the election to the Democratic candidate, this time by his "Raleigh Letter." This historic letter was sent to a friend of Clay's in Alabama, and published by him, and tradition says it was penned under a great white oak in what was lately the yard of Colonel A. B. Andrews on Blount Street. In this letter he advocated the admission of Texas to the Union in due time, and thus set all Abolition New England against his candidacy. He opposed admitting it at once, and thus set his Southern friends against him.

Tradition says that he showed this letter to Judge Badger before he sent it, and that Badger said, "That letter will lose you your candidacy," to which he replied in the often quoted words, "I would rather be right than be president."

In ideals Clay was broadly national, and he was noted as a compromiser, and a soother of men's passions. Personally he was the very ideal man in the imagination of the spirited youth of his day, ideal in faults as well as in virtues.

Christ Church Rectory, once the State Bank, whose first president was Colonel W. Polk. It was one of the first three brick buildings in Raleigh

Old men have told me that since the War they had felt homeless as regarded political affiliation, that they were and had always been "Henry Clay Whigs" and nothing else. Of his great body of adherents it might be said, "His name was all the politics they knew."

Education in the South in those days as obtained by the richer classes was thorough, but there were no standardized secondary schools and scarcely any conception of what they might mean.

The average country citizen of those days was likely to hold the view of Huckleberry Finn's father: "Your father and your mother couldn't read nor write, and you think you are better than your father because you can. I'll take it out of you!" Planters might employ governesses and tutors, and send their children to pay schools, but common people living in rural isolation had no advantages at all in schooling.

Bartlett Yancey is authority for the statement that in Caswell County in 1800 one half the adult white population could not read and write, and that this great proportion grew greater rather than less. In Wake County things must have been better, but how much better we do not know how to discover.

Judge Gaston, in a Fourth of July toast in 1826, speaks of North Carolina as sadly prone in matters educational "to stumble and flounder on at a lazy and lagging pace," and again in 1827, the "Legislature habitually looked with indifference upon education."

A belief among the leaders that this was poor policy was growing each year, and many tentative debates discussing possibilities of establishing common schools were beginning to be held; small appropriations were being laid aside to accumulate looking toward the establishing of an adequate fund for future use; but the fact remained that there was little or no general demand for any sort of free school education up to the year 1840 or '41.

The population of Wake County outside of the city of Raleigh gradually lessened, and became more scattered than formerly through the rural districts. The filling up of the west, which had begun with the century and shortly before, drew thousands of North Carolina people over the turnpikes to Alabama and Tennessee and far away to Missouri and the

EARLY LIFE AND THOUGHT

"New Purchase" as it was called. At the close of the Revolution the population of North Carolina approximated the same number as did that of New York State, but from the war of 1812 until well into the forties, the population of North Carolina was at a comparative standstill.

This emigration, the following of families after their pathfinders, the talk of the golden west and all that, made a great appeal to the imagination of those who stayed behind.

Another great subject for discussion which grew more and more heated was the question of slavery, and attack and defence of this "Institution" was mooted from one end of the United States to the other.

If the cotton gin had lain in the womb of time for another fifty years, slavery in the South might have well become what the doctors call a self-limiting disease and might have followed the course of gradual extinction it had begun in the northern States.

Because of the obvious path of profit, slavery grew from more to more, especially as the south-west was opened up.

New England, always didactic, began to allude first with too much truth to Southern illiteracy, then as time went on to express her conscientious scruples as to the sufferance of slavery in any part of the Union.

Nothing in the general life and thought of the New England states had impressed the South with admiration, the two conceptions of life being at variance. Nothing made our people imagine that moral excellence was greater there than here, and these reproaches were felt undeserved and fell upon ears irritated with constant clash of warring sentiments and opinions. It was as though the sister who lived at home and needed only walk paved streets, should count for a sin the draggled skirts of her whose way had lain through briars and muddy ways.

That New England was the nearest right if not most righteous, was never acknowledged at the South, and in New England the fact of conditions and not deliberate choice was carefully ignored.

Much ink was spilt, and hard sayings on each side grew harder, and anger bred prejudice, and aspersions against slavery made

New England's educational example odious. Justice in this world can never be perfect, but perfect justice is somehow what every man claims for his own. Raleigh, the center of North Carolina's political life, heard many a speech about this bitter controversy, many an echo of the ever growing dispute.

Another subject of prime interest then, as now, was the building of roads, and added to that the projecting of canals. It scarcely seems possible, but the idea was at one time entertained that the City of Raleigh must be connected with the sea by means of the small creeks that run to Neuse River and a system of canals and locks, in connection with that stream, in order to have a commercial outlet.

The State of New York had recently completed the Erie Canal, and the fashion thus set was admired,—this before the days of railroads.

A Scotch engineer engaged for the State by Mr. Peter Brown made calculations on this sort of a plan, on a salary of several times the pay of the Governor. In the early twenties one trip is said to have been made to New Berne and back, with many difficulties. Boat, a scow; captain, James Murray.

The stage coach that brought mail to Raleigh via Louisburg.
(Studied from various old prints and advertisements)

It was calculated that a canal was practical from Hunter's Mill on Walnut Creek, the precise spot of the Waterworks pumping station down to Neuse River, the fall being sufficient, but that a better port would be at the spot near Bloomsbury Park where Lassiter's Mill stands now, and a better canal down Crabtree Creek to the river, though it might have to be longer.

These wild schemes had to be discussed because prices, owing to wagon transportation, were enormous. The salary mark was far, far lower than it is today, and yet calico brought one dollar per yard, broadcloth was worth from seven to ten dollars, and sugar was at the figure of forty-five cents a pound. Nails came by the dozen. Truly it was not the choice of frugality for its elevating charm which influenced our ancestors toward plain living, but necessity, and that of the sternest.

No wonder they listened to fairy tales about easy transportation down Neuse River, where, as today, at some seasons, a terrapin could carry flour on his back all the way from Raleigh to New Berne without wetting his load.

One romantic thing, as we call it now, was part of daily lives then, and we should be glad to experience the thrill ourselves. The stage from the North came in over the Louisburg Road, and went southward to Fayetteville, stopping at Casso's tavern on Fayetteville Street. Three times a week at first it came, then daily. The sweet, flourishing notes of the coach horns could be heard as the lumbering vehicle came into town, and rolled up near the Capitol. This was the link with the world outside. The mail came in, the northern papers with their European news, slowly brought to them in ships, and already more than a month old; letters at fifty and twenty-five cents apiece, according to distance and weight. Strangers would dismount for a moment to stretch their cramped legs a bit, while the fresh horses were put to; or would dismount and spend the night at the tavern.

It was a day's trip from Warrenton to Raleigh, a days' trip from Fayetteville to Raleigh. The passing of the stages was the event of the day, and reminds us of the account in one of Mark Twain's inimitable books of the passing of the New Orleans packet up the river in his youth. If any one had wished to know the census of the able-bodied population of Raleigh, he could doubtless have stepped down from the stage and counted them. Not one would wish to be absent when the stage rolled in.

Of course people read newspapers in those days, and there were good ones, although the sheets were small, and had no sporting page, and no Sunday edition. The editorials were dignified and well written, and compare without disparagement with what we get today, and these weeklies were well read inside and out, as newspapers are not any longer read today, since the armistice.

The Whig paper of the earliest time was called the Raleigh *Minerva*, and was published by William Boylan, the first of the name to come to Raleigh. About six months earlier a paper of rival politics, a Democratic or Jeffersonian organ, was begun by Joseph Gales, an Englishman. He had been driven away from his printing office in Sheffield, England, because of his sympathy with the French Revolution and its very radical developments, such ideas being hateful even to the very mobs, because of the excesses of the Terrorists. He was in some way connected with Doctor

Priestley, who was driven away from Birmingham by mob persecution, a man a hundred years ahead of his time, who also was forced to spend the last of his days in America.

Joseph Gales came to America with Doctor Priestley and was for a time in Philadelphia. Then he came to Raleigh early in the nineteenth century, and the paper he edited here bore the same name as his former journal in Sheffield, "*The Register.*" For many years Joseph Gales was state printer. Besides these two, there was a third sheet, *The Star* which often changed hands, although it was published for years.

As to books, the City of Raleigh in early days was poorly off. Of course some owned a few books, which were read and re-read, and learned almost by heart, to good purpose, and letters and papers of the time show that literary style was far from bad. No books were printed in the state until years later, save a few law books. The list given in Doctor Battle's *History of the University of North Carolina,* of the College library of the first of the century past, will give some idea of the scarcity of all that we should call readable.

Most of the works were heavy and solid enough to kill the largest rat when made into a dead-fall and allowed to drop upon him. Doctor Battle states that this was the use made of Saint Augustine's works in folio and other substantial volumes which were borrowed from the University library for this express purpose. However that may be, there was little to read in Raleigh then but law, classics and theology, with a very few novels which were heavy to hold if not to read. I have before me a copy of *"Sir Charles Grandison,"* owned in Raleigh in 1813 or '14, which is as large as a family Bible, has two columns of rather small print, and seven hundred pages. This light work was a reprint from the seven volumes originally issued, and is dated 1810, printed in London.

The eating and drinking which built up life from its physical side was much like the food of today, and yet unlike in many ways.

Chicago beef was not to be had, nor was there an abattoir, nor an ice plant. Local supplies were all that obtained, and much more pork and bacon was used by all classes. Vegetables were raised the same as now, but

"Casso's Tavern" as it looked in the olden time. It was the second brick building in Raleigh, corner Fayetteville and Morgan Streets

the cow pea was considered food for beasts alone, and the useful tomato was unknown. Canning was a thing unpracticed, although dried fruit was plentifully used. A little "pound for pound" preserves for state occasions was kept on hand from year to year. Sugar was scarce and molasses of the home-grown sort took the place of it. The imported molasses was most delicious, being far better than it has been since, and was the accepted sweetening for many foods. Hospitality laid stress on one sort of refreshment that is but a sad memory to the thirsty. Imported and domestic wines and liquors were used in great variety, and every gentleman considered it his duty to have such things on hand for the chance guest, however he might prefer to abstain himself. Hence the mahogany cellarets which still grace many old fashioned dining rooms, and the portly glass decanters which are now set back on the china-closet shelves, but used to stand out within reach.

As regards the furniture that we are still carefully collecting, are we not sure that the things then bought and admired are still the most beautiful that are obtainable? Do we not regard thus all old sofas and desks and secretaires and what not?

Has there ever been more satisfactory silverware than the gracefully shaped spoons and pierced fruit baskets that we treasure with pride and buy now and then for great prices?

Household work was far greater then than it is now, and the notable housewife must be like Solomon's virtuous woman in her ceaseless activities. Providing work and supervision for the many and lazy servants made her rise early and be ceaselessly busy. Even Colonel Byrd, though not enthusiastic about the men, acknowledges that the women of early North Carolina were a thrifty race, and we may be sure that they knew how to sew and knit and dye and weave and embroider and care for meats and supervise all the varied domestic arts.

It is interesting to note that in the twenties and the thirties young folk were considered very mannerless and unmanageable.

The spinning of "street yarn" was much deprecated, the extreme idleness of young men was censured in private letters and in the newspapers, and older folk were caused much anxiety by the strange tendency of the young girls to dress up and go out gadding when there was work for them to do at home!

All these many things, great and small, go to make up the tenor of the lives of our forerunners. Sometimes the small are more important than the great in filling up the many details which add most to the picture, and it is a picture that I am trying, awkwardly perhaps, but anxiously, to place before your eyes.

CHAPTER VI.

Giants of Those Days

COLONEL WILLIAM POLK, coming from Mecklenburg County to Raleigh very early in its history, was a figure of great prominence here, and would still have been were his adoptive city a far larger place. He came of that well known Polk family which lived in Mecklenburg before the Revolution, and was cousin to President Polk. In his youth he was an eye-witness to the signing of the Mecklenburg Declaration of Independence, and it is so stated in the Life of Leonidas K. Polk. He enlisted in the Continental Army when a mere boy and was in active service all through the Revolutionary War. He was twice wounded, very severely at the battle of Germantown. He suffered that sad winter at Valley Forge with Washington, and he was also present with him at Yorktown.

He was twice married, his first wife dying before he came to Raleigh. His second wife was a Miss Hawkins of Warrenton, in Warren

County. She bore him nine children of whom the second was Leonidas K. Polk.

Colonel Polk came to Raleigh in the year 1799 to become the first president of the State Bank, serving without compensation. His home was a large house which used to close the end of Blount Street just as the Centennial School now closes Fayetteville Street. It was standing ten years ago, and was used for a while after the war for a girls' school.

The old State Bank where Colonel Polk presided is now used for the Rectory of Christ Church and is the third brick building which was erected in Raleigh, the first one being the old State House, the second Casso's Hotel, now used for stores and some of the State offices, at the corner of Morgan and Fayetteville, still sturdy and substantial. The State Bank building was much laughed at, in the early day, because it was considered queer architecture. One can still trace the newer bricks where the old Bank door was built up on the New Berne Avenue side. "Two porches, and a house between, like the ham sandwich."

Colonel Polk of those days was a tall stately imposing figure, of old-fashioned formal manner, and ceremonious dignity, but capable of unbending genially on occasion. He was a citizen for everyone to be proud of, the man whom his neighbors honored and called upon to welcome distinguished guests and be the presiding genius of public meetings and toastmaster at banquets on state occasions. In politics he was an old time Federalist, but in his youth he had a boy friend, a neighbor in Mecklenburg County whose name was Andrew Jackson.

The halo which surrounded this venerable Revolutionary figure grew brighter as time went on and thinned the ranks of his fellow soldiers and the story of their deeds became a sort of legend. At his death he was probably the last survivor of the Revolutionary officers in all North Carolina.

Colonel Polk, like other gentlemen of his time, was a convivial soul, as no one thought harm of being; but he was no vulgar roysterer and he took a firm stand against duelling, then an accepted way of protecting "honor" and settling controversies. On one occasion he wrote for publication a strong letter condemning the practice, and this had great weight because it was from a man so well known to be of distinguished courage. This declaration was needed, as at least one duel had been fought about that time by a Wake County man.

Alfred Jones of White Plains was a party in a duel about 1820, and was badly wounded. He always declared that though he nearly died of his wound, he considered the mental anguish he suffered for a few seconds while looking down his opponent's murderous pistol-barrel was more grim and unforgetable than the physical pain of the wound. He felt his honor entirely less satisfied.

To return to Colonel Polk. He was one of those who owned great tracts of land in Tennessee, and was once making a trip into that state on business connected with his property, when he saw, leaning over a fence beside his road, a man whom he at once recognized, and whom he knew only too well. It was a Tory, who had formerly lived neighbor to his father in Mecklenburg, and who had taken an opportunity while the men of the family were away in the army to wreck and plunder his father's plantation. The Colonel, knowing him for this deed and knowing that he had got off scot free, handed his horse's rein to his companion, and without one word, dismounted and fell like an avalanche upon the astonished man, giving him a horsewhipping that was entirely consoling to the giver, as well as fully satisfying to the recipient. State Treasurer Haywood was the authority for this anecdote.

Another story tells of his showing the young folk how to dance a minuet in the stately fashion of the eighteenth century, Miss Betsy Geddy of the statue-saving fame being his *vis-a-vis* and dancing partner.

When his son Leonidas, just graduated from West Point, insisted upon resigning from the army to study for the Episcopal ministry, Colonel Polk could neither understand nor become resigned to it. It is said that he spoke of it for some time with an oath whenever he mentioned it.

Cousin to one President of the United States, friend of another, Colonel Polk was the man who chanced to put a bit of bread into the mouth of a third. Jacob Johnson, father of Andrew Johnson, Lincoln's successor in the Presidency, was for many years porter and factotum at the State Bank, under Colonel Polk, and afterward.

This man Johnson was absolutely uneducated, but Governor Swain describes his quick heroism in saving Mr. T. Henderson from drowning in Hunter's pond, according to account by William Peace. It was at a picnic, and the canoe overset and Henderson was unable to swim. Johnson lived in a small house near Casso's Hotel. Miss Margaret Casso named the future President Andrew Jackson, although he afterward dropped the middle name. A newspaper advertisement is still in existence offering a reward for the return of this Raleigh boy to his legal guardians, when he ran away from his apprenticeship at about twelve years of age.

Successor to Colonel Polk at the State Bank was William Boylan, the first of the name. He was editor of the Raleigh *Minerva*, sometime state printer, and he was also a rich planter, dying worth a million dollars at the time when millionaires were most unusual and money was far more valuable. Mr Boylan came originally from New Jersey, but had kin in North Carolina. His portrait shows a face of a very different character from the others of that gallery. He looks, among those great lawyers, like a sedate business man and his qualities of mind were the prophecy of coming times. Mr. Boylan was public-spirited and progressive. He first saw the possibilities, and set the example of raising great quantities of cotton on the uplands of Wake. Whitney's cotton gin had made the growing of cotton profitable because the gin could remove the seed from a thousand pounds of cotton in a day, which labor previously had to be done slowly and tediously by hand. Also the invention of the power-driven loom and spinning machinery made more cotton necessary to keep the looms of the world at work, and the development of the necessary inventions had built up a mighty industry. Mr. Boylan planted acres of cotton where square rods had been the custom before. He also became interested in transportation, and a heavy investor in our first railroads. He was at one time president of the Raleigh and Gaston Railroad. Governor Swain says of him that he was dignified and grave, and it also is sure that he must have been charitable, for he is responsible for the building of the first county poor-house in Wake. Before that the County poor were boarded out with the lowest bidder at county expense; a hard arrangement.

Doctor Kemp Battle, from whose centennial address many details of this old time may be gathered, tells a story of how Mr. Boylan sent loads of wood around to the poor, caught as they were without fuel in the time of the wonderful "big snow of '57." He states that one "son of rest" keeping warm abed that coldest morning, humped up in his mound of bedding to inquire whether Mr. Boylan "had had that wood cut up to fit his fireplace before it was loaded on the wagon?"

Mr. Boylan lived in the Joel Lane house which he had bought from Peter Brown. But one undignified thing is told of him—that is his part in the fight which he and Joseph Gales, rival editors, fought about some political question. In this Mr. Gales was worsted, and brought suit for damages, which were awarded to the sum of two hundred dollars, which amount he donated to the Academy.

"White Plains," the country home of the Jones Family of the southeast side of the county. A remnant of one of the famous oaks, of which there once were four diverging avenues.

The two worthy combatants were afterward reconciled and shook hands in token of amity. Mr. Boylan died in 1859, his life thus spanning the whole time of industrial and material growth before the war.

Peter Brown, Esquire, was a lawyer and a bachelor. He came to Raleigh in the first years of its existence, but in his old age he wished to return to Scotland, or thought he did; so he sold his property, including the historic Joel Lane house as above, and went back across the water. He had contracted the Raleigh habit however, and matter of fact as he appeared, he let sentiment take him back to Scotland, and then bring him back again to North Carolina, where he died after all.

Peter Brown also took a turn at being president of the State Bank. He knew something of the Scotch ideas of banking, said to be the best at that time. He was a lawyer of ability as well as a financier, and was for some time the only practicing attorney in Raleigh. His oddity was great as his ability. Once he found occasion to move his law office, and when ready for business in the new quarters, he hung out the following notice: "Peter Brown, Attorney at Law, has moved from where he was, to where he now is; where he may henceforth at all times be found." No ambiguity in that!

Judge Seawell, nephew of Nathaniel Macon, was one of the legal lights of the time. He married a daughter of James Hinton, son of Colonel John the first, and his descendants live here still. He was a well-known lawyer and citizen representing this county in the Assembly several terms.

Moses Mordecai, the first of the family of legal and other prominence, came to Raleigh in time to buy a lot at the second city sale. Only recently has the great square, with the old mansion built far back upon it, been finally divided into smaller lots. Mr. Mordecai's first and second wives were sisters, Margaret and Annie Lane, daughters of Joel Lane. Many of their descendants are among us now.

One of the old time merchants was William Peck, who did a banking and mercantile business at the south-east corner of the Capitol facing Wilmington Street. He was a hatter by trade, a safe man and a good citizen. He admired the new Capitol as it gradually rose from foundation to dome and watched its progress day by day from his shop door, complaining mightily when the grading up of the square began, and because of the bank of earth in front of him he could no longer see the whole building in its entirety. Like Judge Cloud of State-wide fame, he disliked whistling as a means of self-expression, and of course all the small boys of Raleigh took care to make a long, shrill, ear-piercing effort, just as they rounded his corner on a dead run. A story is told of him, a legend which is a sort of classical myth of the days of private banks of issue, and which is printed in that old book, "*Flush Times in Alabama and Mississippi,*" a story which may be true, but is at any rate a good parable, and runs this way:

A Mississippi horse-trader wanted to buy exchange on North Carolina, and bargained for a draft on Mr. Peck's banking institution. His exchange cost him ten dollars a thousand. Then the banker in Mississippi asked if his customer would do him the favor of carrying a small package with him to North Carolina to be delivered to his "old friend, Peck."

The trader easily consented to do this. On arrival in Raleigh he presented his draft, and Mr. Peck was most positive that he owed the bank in Mississippi nothing, but would like to look over his books and make sure. As he turned to go, the trader handed the package to Mr. Peck, with the message, and when unsealed, it contained the North Carolina bills necessary to offset the draft. The trader had paid ten dollars a thousand for his exchange, and then had taken the risk of bringing his own money that long, dangerous way besides. This is a good story to illustrate the working of the banking methods in vogue before railroads and national banks were in existence.

Jokes are the most difficult things to transplant out of the time that gives them being, but there is an old joke which might be told here, connected with Mr. Peck. It is a true tale, well avouched this time. One night the great beaver, twice natural size, which swung over the door of his shop and was his sign, disappeared unaccountably. Next morning a student at the University appeared in chapel with this hat balanced on his head and further disguised with huge goggles and a long coat, with a cane in hand. This brought down the house and broke up prayers for that morning, as it might well have done with several hundred young scapegraces fairly pining for an excuse for a demonstration. The naughty boy who stole the hatter's sign was named R. S. Tucker, and, in partnership with his brother, became a considerable merchant himself in after days. The father, Ruffin Tucker, had settled in Raleigh some years before this and was by trade a printer. Descendants of this man are among those successful in business of the city.

Dr. McPheeters, who has already been mentioned as head of the Academy and as "Town Pastor," was a very interesting figure of old Raleigh. He took his calling in dead earnest, and ruled on week days and on Sundays continuously, so that the boy who played hooky and went fishing on Sunday instead of to church and Sunday School, was made to regret his mistake when he reached day-school Monday morning.

Once Dr. McPheeters was about to visit the sins of his youth in this way upon the future Bishop of Louisiana, and Lonnie Polk

The birthplace of Andrew Johnson, President of the United States. This shows it on its second location. It is now at Pullen Park.

broke away and ran for it. He was instantly pursued, caught, and birched by the Doctor who on that occasion laid down the law in an axiom which is old but by no means obsolete. "No boy," said Dr. McPheeters, "who is not old enough to behave properly when he knows he has been fairly warned, is too old to be whipped for misbehavior."

The Peace brothers were men of diligence and probity, successful merchants. William left a sum for the building of Peace Institute. They were both bachelors, and their name suited their character. One of the city streets is named after them.

I have mentioned Joseph Gales and his establishing the first newspaper, also his connection by birth and association with the ferment of new thought in the manufacturing districts of middle England. After his printing office was wrecked and he was driven to emigrate, he came from Philadelphia to Raleigh. He was a man of resources, bringing some capital with him, and having the knowledge needful to start a paper mill to supply his press.

His wife, Mrs Winifred Gales, was highly educated and had ability. She wrote the first novel that was ever written and printed in North Carolina, although not many have been produced since. We have never caught the writer's itch; however, it may some day come to us. She is "the first that ever burst" into the "silent sea" of North Carolina authorship. She died in 1839, her husband two years later. They lie buried in the old City Cemetery. Beside their graves are those of two grown daughters lost a few years earlier, victims to one of those recurring epidemics of malaria that took toll of so many who did not know that mosquitoes and a prevailing southerly wind over Hunter's pond on Walnut Creek were the combined cause of so much chills and fever in the town of Raleigh. The Gales have still descendants living in Raleigh and claiming the city as home.

David L. Swain lies buried in Oakwood Cemetery, and he lived his formative years here, although he was chiefly known by his later work as President of the University of North Carolina. As a young man he came to Raleigh, and studied law with Chief Justice Taylor, who married the only sister of Judge Gaston.

Although born in Buncombe County, and coming to Wake after he was a man grown, Swain was near akin to the Lanes and other families connected with them; his mother being Caroline, sister of Joel Lane, and he being the son by her second husband, named as they say after the first, David Lowrie.

Not many educational advantages came to this lad in the western wilds, and young Swain had scanty schooling, and but four months of university instruction, before he went to Raleigh to study law. Every crumb of learning that came his way he seized and assimilated, and every book which he laid his hands upon he read, especially absorbing all obtainable history. Though his early life was not so sordid and pinched as that of Abraham Lincoln, yet his education and development bear some likeness to that of Lincoln, because he was like him, a rough diamond, and took polish from all the friction of later life; and because his education was in progress all during that later life.

When he had won his law license he returned to Buncombe, and was immediately sent to represent that county in the next Assembly.

Here he attended to the important bill introduced by him, for building the French Broad Turnpike, leading west into Tennessee. In 1829, he received an odd compliment, being elected Solicitor for the Edenton District because factional fighting had become desperately bitter, and only a man from outside the district could be tolerated. Next he was appointed Judge of the Superior Court, and was chosen over Henry Seawell, of Raleigh, a man of greater known distinction and a most excellent lawyer. His judgeship was but another step upward.

He was elected Governor of North Carolina by the Legislature, as was the constitutional provision at that time, and was re-elected for two succeeding years. During his term as Governor he represented Buncombe County in the Constitutional Convention of 1836. This Convention was to change the Constitution of North Carolina in many details, and among other matters to amend the laws governing the representation of the different sections of the State in the Assembly. Governor Swain was full of detailed information regarding the State's history and statistics, from the earliest Colonial times, and he led the reform party which equalized differences between the east and the west—matters which had never been adjusted, and which had stirred up strife between the sections ever since the Revolution.

In this same year, Doctor Joseph Caldwell, President of the University, died, and Governor Swain asked his friend Judge Nash whether he could recommend him for appointment to the vacancy. Judge Nash thought, naturally enough, of formal academic education, and of the lack of such preparation which Governor Swain's exclusively political life must present. All that he would promise was to consult Judge Cameron about the request. The latter held a different opinion. He declared that Governor Swain had all necessary requisites for the position except formal scholarship; that he had always been able to manage men, and should know well how to manage boys, and that his education, while not conventional, was far broader than might be supposed.

At the next meeting of the Board of Trustees Swain was elected President of the University and went to Chapel Hill to take up his

Home built by Captain Wiatt, about 1815, Hillsborough Road, near Raleigh. This is now near the highway shops.

real crowning life-work. Hence some humorist has said that the State of North Carolina had given him every office in her power, and had at last sent him to college to get an education. This was an unjust taunt to a man so well self-taught, and whose cultivation was a progressive process lasting all his life. He himself was the Historical Society, and his collections of documents were very complete for that early time. The historian Bancroft used his collections and consulted his knowledge for the chapters in his History of the United States which concern North Carolina. Governor Swain's political strength had been aided greatly by his unerring memory for kinship, names and dates, and this gift also helped him in his knowledge and management of his boys. His legal power was founded on his grasp of detail, and by this also he was fitted to record the history of the State he loved.

Papers in the University Magazine, by his hand, and a few occasional addresses full of dry humor, are all that he left as formal writings of a historical nature, and these are all too few; but they give a presentment of the life that then was, on the far side of that bloody chasm which was to divide all our history in twain.

Like Judge Gaston, Governor Swain was a Federalist in politics, and became later a Whig. He married Eleanor White of Raleigh, the daughter of William White, Secretary of State, and a grand-daughter of Governor Caswell. He died in 1868, some say of grief over the wreck of his beloved University, accomplished in the disheartening Reconstruction days. In person he was a tall, awkward man, one of those whose appearance lends point to some humorous nick-name. His students called Governor Swain "Old Bunk," referring to his native county.

It is only in Governor Swain's reminiscences of Raleigh that we gather the traits of the lesser folk, lesser only in not being conspicuous as State officials. He mentions and characterizes many, of whom we may mention Mr. Casso, the Italian tavern keeper whose descendants are many, Dugald McKeithan who married a Lane, the cousin of the Governor, John Meares, James McKee, Benjamin King, Captain, afterwards Sheriff Wyatt, the first member of the Briggs family, the original David Royster, cabinet-maker (this last was in Raleigh by 1801), John Stewart who married Miss Margaret Casso and is the ancestor of the Binghams of Mebane, James Coman, a Frenchman, the Smiths, substantial merchants, whose heir, Miss Mary Smith, afterwards Mrs. Morehead, left her money to the University, Ruffin Tucker who has been mentioned, who worked for twenty-five dollars a *year* and board during his first year in Raleigh.

John Rex, the tanner, will be mentioned more fully later. One John S. Raboteau, a French Huguenot, a saddler by trade, should be named here, for his grand-daughter married A. F. Page, and through her he is ancestor of the great Ambassador to England, and his brothers, builders of North Carolina. Sheriff Page, recently dead, was of kin to these.

Also there was a Captain Wiatt who built the house on Hillsborough road where the Highway Commission's great shops stand today, and who was the Marshall of the Supreme Court for many years. He came from Virginia, was a veteran of 1812, and built a country home almost like the one of about the same epoch belonging to General Calvin Jones, his comrade in arms. Captain Wiatt had a wayside well which was used by all the passers-by. He was also celebrated for the kindness of his heart and the great freedom of his command of bad language. He was one of those who swore terribly, although this is all that was ever said in his dispraise. His home has been very long a landmark of the county.

CHAPTER VII
More Biographies

N a previous chapter we sketched Colonel William Polk, the Revolutionary hero who was so much the leading citizen of Raleigh for so many years, and for the completion of the story of our best example of character transmitted from father to son and built up in the Raleigh of old time, we shall add a life of his son, Leonidas, who became the celebrated Bishop-Brigadier of the Confederate Army.

We are not able to claim possession of that great "Revolutionary Titan," as Governor Swain calls John Marshall, who rode his circuit as United States Justice, and was thus a regular visitor to Raleigh, riding alone from Richmond all those dreary miles in his gig. The trip took him a week. We may retell, however, the stories still remembered of him, of his simplicity, his kindly good nature, of how he loved to pitch horseshoes with the townsfolk, of afternoons when court had adjourned; of how once he could get no tailor to make him a pair of new breeches, for love nor money, because he would not ask him to take away the turn already promised to a customer to serve himself. As Justice Marshall would not insist upon any special consideration he had at that time to hold court in ragged breeches, which made no more difference than he thought it did, namely, no difference at all.

Swain says, "I shall never see nor hear his like again," and Judge Badger tells of Marshall's saying in his hearing, "The Constitution of the United States is to be construed not loosely, not strictly, but honestly." Here you see Judge Badger learning those lessons of moderation and of justice which he put to good use for himself in his later life.

State Treasurers are usually retained for many successive years; Secretaries of State for long terms, also being re-elected and passing their lives with us and becoming permanent residents. The Judges of the Supreme Court of North Carolina did not do this so invariably, while Governors, having short terms of office, were more often but transient sojourners. Men from other states often came to us. The mention of such solid and worthy qualities as those of Duncan Cameron and Kenneth Rayner, might be made as examples of the great gain which often came to this city and state when such men chose to cast in their lot among us.

It is said that you must have been a part of the city of Charleston for three generations before you can claim to belong to the place. Raleigh has been more hospitable from the first, and has added to herself many a good and worthy man by this virtue.

Certainly Judge Gaston should be characterized in any story of Wake County. His memory deserves honor among us for what he was enabled to accomplish for Raleigh as well as for his great service to the State.

He was born in New Berne, and when living in Raleigh inhabited a little office building in the yard of that house which stood, until a few years ago, at the south-west corner of Salisbury and West Hargett Streets. This was originally the home of Chief Justice Taylor, who married Judge Gaston's sister. The little office in question was on the very corner, and stood in an old fashioned garden, under a huge ginkgo tree, and with vines and flowers about its rear. Business houses have encroached on this old residence, and brick and mortar entirely cover its site today.

Judge Gaston has no living relatives in the State. His portraits, both painted and chiseled in marble, are to be seen in the State Library building. That he was a very great lawyer those who know affirm enthusiastically; that he was a greater man, a white-souled Galahad of his day, his contemporaries agree in testifying, while his letters bear it out. "His Sanctity" as one reverent admirer calls him. Judge Gaston's pictured face is intellectual, calm, regular in feature, but shows a sad expression of the mouth, a somewhat pathetic air. Gaston is said to have been a bit too fine-grained for the rough game of politics. He could not hate any one with his whole heart for a moment, not even one of another party! His high standards and personal ideals joined with his judicial temperament, made some things unbearable to him which would scarce have provoked a shrug from a less sensitive man. When the Federalist Party went to pieces he felt a little homeless politically, and registers his disappointment in his advice to Governor Swain never to be persuaded to re-enter public life after he had found useful retirement away from it.

Judge Gaston was first a Congressman, retiring to practice law but going to the State Senate from time to time. In 1833 he was appointed to the Supreme Court after the death of Judge Leonard Henderson.

In religion he was a Catholic, and used his influence in the Constitutional Convention of 1835 to do away with the restraints on religious liberty and amend the Constitution to read "Christian," instead of "Protestant," when enumerating the qualifications for public office. His speeches on that theme are said to have carried his hearers deep into the realm of abstract justice, leaving mere expediency far behind.

In this connection let it be stated that in the Constitutional Convention of 1861 the last religious limitation was removed, when disabilities were removed from the Jews, by ordinance introduced by William Johnston of Mecklenburg, father to Mrs. A. B. Andrews, whose memorial volume this is intended to become.

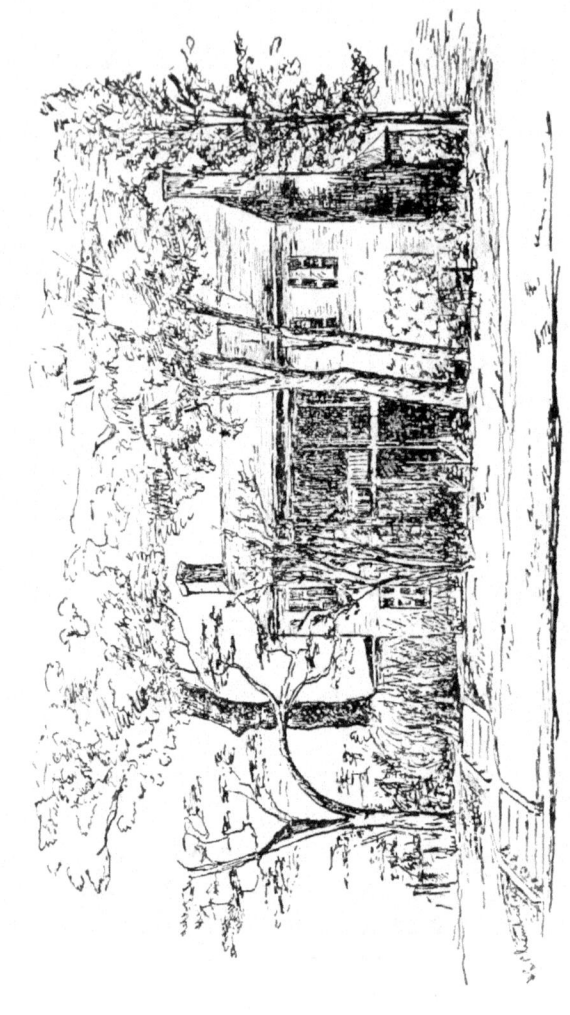

The Burke Haywood mansion on New Berne Avenue built by Treasurer John Haywood before 1800

Judge Gaston's celebrated eloquence, like that of many another dead orator, is hard to estimate at this time. His speeches are dignified, sensible, patterned with metaphors like the figures on an old-fashioned brocade, and like it a bit stiff. Voice and intonation are gone. Great oratory is a fading flower. Gaston's signal service to us and to Raleigh was his determining influence in persuading the Legislature to retain the Capital of the State on the old site. In doing this he kept our heritage for us which might have been lost but for him. He was the author of the words of our State song, "Carolina, Carolina, Heaven's blessings attend her!" He was also permitted in that heated time to speak many wise words about slavery, to prophesy its downfall, and all this without offense, such was the universal respect for his purity and sincerity. His taking off was very sudden. His last words were a confession of faith in God and Christianity.

We have mentioned the name of John Haywood, State Treasurer for forty years, builder of the venerable mansion which stands unchanged on New Berne Avenue and shelters his descendants. He came to Raleigh in the year 1787, and about that same time three brothers of his also settled here: Henry, father of Senator William H. Haywood, Sherwood Haywood, and Stephen Haywood. By prominence of position and by services the Treasurer was the best known of the four. His portrait shows a handsome, well marked face with dark eyes and a smiling expression, crowned with a mass of prematurely grey hair. He was an able man, but his greatest talent was the art of doing kind things kindly. He was a veritable genius at friendship.

Besides the duties of his office, he interested himself in the infant University, and he is said to have missed not more than two trustees' meetings in his whole career, a signal devotion when we consider the long muddy miles that had to be wallowed through on horseback for nearly a whole day, both going and coming, to the winter meetings. It is a persistent tradition that he was the designer of the seal and motto of the University. This has not been established, but it is given for its intrinsic likelihood.

He was responsible for calling to Raleigh that good and useful man Dr. William McPheeters who was a native of Virginia, and who became both schoolmaster and town pastor and was long a kind of Presbyterian Pope of Raleigh.

Each session of the Legislature, Mr. Haywood invited each member to eat at least one meal with him, and he knew more men well and pleasantly than did any other man in the State unless it may have been Governor Swain.

His funeral was a state affair, with full military honors, and though Mr. Haywood was an Episcopalian in denomination, his old friend Dr. McPheeters pronounced the funeral discourse, closing with these words: "Integrity and innocence were his guardian angels, and out of the furnace of suspicion he came unhurt." Haywood County, where Waynesville is situated, was named for our longest incumbent in the Treasurer's office.

Judge Badger was one of the ablest men ever produced in North Carolina. He was born in the eastern part of the State, and was a precocious genius, graduating from Yale University very young. By the time he was thirty years old, he had been a lawyer, a congressman, and a judge, and had left the bench to practice law in Raleigh.

William Peace, the merchant, told of having sold him a suit of black broadcloth on credit, when he was just twenty years old and had, at that early age, obtained his law license. It was against his custom, he said, but he was so taken with the gallant youth, that he risked the money upon him without security, and was entirely justified in doing so.

Judge Badger had still a long and a brilliant career before him after he settled in Raleigh. When the Whig party rose out of the ruins of the Federalist, after the disputes with Jackson, Badger was appointed Secretary of the Navy under Harrison. When Tyler, after succeeding to the presidential chair on Harrison's death, split the party, Badger resigned his portfolio along with the rest of the cabinet. Soon after this he succeeded William H. Haywood as Senator, serving until 1855. Always a man of great brilliancy of mind he took hold of nothing by the rough handle. It was a criticism of him that he was too jocular, that he could make a joke of anything and laugh it out of court. He held well-defined opinions, however, and was a moderate man, a conciliator. In his opinions about slavery he followed the ideas and the hopes of Henry Clay.

In denomination he was Episcopalian, and was an active opponent of Bishop Ives, who was touched with a wave of that same belief which was troubling the Church of England at that time, and which carried Newman over into the Catholic Church. That was also the final development with Bishop Ives, and Badger early recognized whither this Romanizing tendency was drifting, and opposed and exposed the change in the conventions of the Episcopal Church.

A staunch Union man, a moderate and a conservative, Judge Badger was nevertheless forced by the cruel turn of affairs in '61 to move the secession ordinance, as representing Wake County, in May of that year. He died in '66. His second wife was a sister of Leonidas Polk, and his third wife was a Haywood.

Like the Polks and like the Haywoods, the Battles have given good men and faithful ones to Raleigh. Judge Battle, father of Doctor Kemp Battle, so long President of the University and historian of it, father also of our late useful townsman Richard Battle, Esquire, lived for most of his active years in Raleigh. Duncan Cameron moved here in 1829 and was chairman of the committee which had charge of the building of the second Capitol; he also had charge of the building of Christ Church, thus leaving his mark on Raleigh in these lovely buildings. He was also president of the the State Bank until succeeded later by his son-in-law, George Mordecai.

Leonidas Polk, the second son of Colonel William Polk, was born in Raleigh. In a former chapter he has been characterized as a live boy, a student at the old Academy under Dr. McPheeters. His distinctive accomplishment as a youth was his gift of song. He could sing more old songs better than anyone else in town.

When prepared he went early to Chapel Hill, remaining two years. A part of that time Governor Swain was his room-mate. In 1822 he received his appointment to West Point.

Up to this time in his life he was a high-spirited and care-free but ambitious lad, having perhaps a keener pair of eyes in his head than most, and indeed he was scarcely more than twenty when he entered the Military Academy.

There he encountered an atmosphere as devoid of any religious warmth as an institution could manifest without being absolutely atheistic or openly vicious in its influence. It is not known to the average person what a tendency to irreligion was shown in our country during the early part of the last century, before the great revivals began to sweep their converts into the churches, and before a true missionary spirit became active. The older folk of that time were of the generation of the French Revolution, and the most educated minds, like Jefferson's for example, were full of the ideas of Voltaire or of Tom Paine, and were often agnostic in refusing to fix any religious belief.

At West Point at that time it was considered soft and silly to notice the subject of religion in any way. Not a single officer there was a professor of any religious faith at that time, although they had a chaplain for form's sake. About that time a new chaplain was appointed and came to serve them. He records how chilling he found the apathy and the veiled scorn he met, but he was the kind of man whose conviction led him to strive to accomplish something under any conditions. He

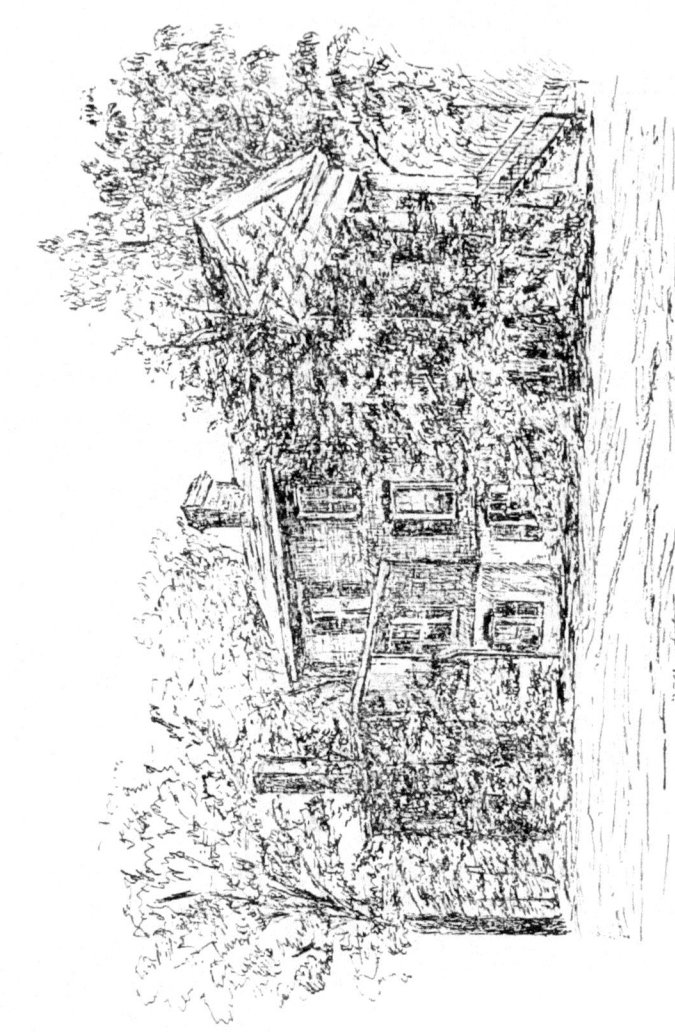

"Wills Forest," old Devereux place, built in 1830 and torn down to make way for the suburb of Glenwood

was able to influence Leonidas Polk, and made in him his first convert. The young man was deeply and genuinely touched and changed. After graduating at West Point, he told his father of his new outlook and of his recently taken decision to leave the army and study for the Church. While Colonel Polk's plans for his boy were cruelly frustrated, still there was no open breach between them, and the father became more reconciled as time passed. After studying at the seminary in Alexander, Virginia, Leonidas was ordained deacon in 1831.

Before that time he had married Miss Devereux, daughter of John Devereux of Raleigh, and when a few years later he was consecrated Missionary Bishop of the Southwest, he moved to Tennessee to the generous tract his father allotted him of a thousand acres of good blue grass.

The diocese of the new bishop was enormous consisting of Alabama, Mississippi, Louisiana, Arkansas, Indian Territory of Oklahoma, and the great state of Texas. The whole of this wide extent of country was still sparsely settled, and its isolated inhabitants had very little religious instruction and did not wish for any. In emigrating, they had escaped restraint, and unlike the more northern emigrants they were mostly country people and did not come from communities well organized religiously. Their old homes had often been as isolated to all intents and purposes as the new ones so far on the frontier.

This made the problem of the missionary, and on one of his long journeys a Texan told Bishop Polk that he was wasting his time. "Go home; go home, young man," said this man earnestly, "we are not worth saving!"

An anecdote told of one of these border ruffians of this decade will illustrate the lawless undisciplined spirit of the South-west with which Bishop Polk had to deal in the beginning of his ministry. It was a man who had been jailed for manslaughter and was most indignant, considering it an outrage, and saying, "Now-a-days you can't put an inch or so of knife into a fellow, or lam him over the head with a stick of wood, but every little lackey must poke his nose in, and law, law, law is the word. Then after the witnesses swear to their pack o'lies, and the lawyers get their jaw in, that old cuss that sets up there high and grinds out the law to 'em, he must have his how-de-do! I tell you I won't stay in no such a country. I mean to go to Texas, where a man can have some peace and not be interfered with in his private concerns!"

This was the spirit that Bishop Polk met over and over again in his long journeys all over this great district. His life was threatened with violence in more than one frontier place, but he was a man who could not be daunted; and beside this he well understood the tempers and manners of his southern fellow-countrymen. He did the work of an evangelist with much success. Later he helped to initiate and organize the University of the South at Sewanee, Tennessee.

The war came on in '61, and Jefferson Davis, President of the Confederacy, being in need of all the trained soldiers possible to lead and train his armies, asked his advisers if they supposed Bishop Polk would allow himself to be appointed Major-General. This appointment was offered to him, without his having any surmise of it beforehand. After some consideration, Bishop Polk accepted the commission, and served his country and chosen cause as Major, afterwards Brigadier-General all through the war. Quite late in the struggle he was killed during the fighting round Atlanta. He was buried in Augusta, Georgia.

His men called him Bishop more often than they called him General, and he was much loved. He kept his sacred calling well to the fore, while doing the difficult duty of a soldier and officer in command.

Such a sincere picturesque figure as he makes is a worthy subject for study and interest. We cannot claim many such distinguished and unusual persons.

Many soldiers went out from Raleigh and of these many distinguished themselves. Their histories are part of that great book of golden deeds which should be read as long as books are made. But it would be too long to try to tell of them all; to tell of those who came home alive to work out a restoration of the piteous destruction of war, and of those who were mercifully spared the further sacrifice except the one of their lives given in a moment of time, rather than spent painfully day by day. These things will be better told by others. There is not room here for that long roll of heroic names.

CHAPTER VIII

Improvements and Progress

SOMETIMES improvement is definitely started by the stimulation of a great loss. The Raleigh that we know today only began to come into existence after the old town had been destroyed by a series of fires.

Of these the most serious and the most spectacular was the burning of the old State House in 1831. From Governor Swain's account, given as an eye-witness, we can recall the despair and dismay of this loss.

The fire occurred in broad daylight, the middle of a summer day, June 21st, 1831, and caught from a solder pot which a careless workman took into the loft where he was repairing something about the roof, and there left it, while he went to dinner. During his absence the fire caught and spread unnoticed.

Once before, in 1799, there had been an alarm about fire, a warning given by Andrew Jackson, conveyed to his old friend and for-

182   HISTORY OF WAKE COUNTY

mer neighbor Colonel Polk, to the effect that it was conspired to destroy the State House in that way. It seems that the Secretary of State, Glasgow, holding his office as a respected leader and a Revolutionary officer of repute, had somehow fallen into bad ways, and was issuing fraudulent land warrants. The deception being found out, he was prosecuted, and to prevent conviction he had designed to burn the State House, and with it all evidences of his crime. This plot Jackson discovered, and the State House and its records were saved, while Glasgow fled from justice.

This time, however, the fire was well under way before anyone knew about it, and when the flames appeared they were at the top of the building, and there was not even a ladder at hand long enough to reach the trouble. And so that bright June day, the State House burned leisurely, the black smoke rolled up into the blue sky while the owls and bats and flying squirrels scurried out of the burning dome in panic, and the terrified people of Raleigh ran helplessly to and fro across the Capitol Square. Mr Hill, Secretary of State, had ample time to save the State papers. A few that were lost at that time were afterwards restored by bequest of Waightstill Avery, from his private collections.

Miss Betsy Geddy, that spirited and gritty maiden lady, rallied all comers to try and move the Canova statue of Washington from beneath the burning roof. The citizens took hold, under her leadership and encouragement, and tried hard, but the marble was very heavy, and there were not hands enough to lift or to move it. There remained nothing to do but to watch it burn. By and by the fire had surrounded it, and it could be seen heated red-hot, glowing like a figure in a fiery furnace. So it shone for a time with unearthly beauty, and suddenly the roof fell in upon it and it broke and crumbled in utter and final ruin. A silence fell on the watching throng, and some little child's voice was heard speaking the sorrow of all: "Poor State House, poor statue, I'm so sorry!"

After the smoking ruins in the Capitol Square had been quenched in a few summer rains, the question was asked and the discussion began whether the edifice should or should not be rebuilt in the same spot or another Capital city selected.

At the next General Assembly the controversy became hot. Fayetteville, always sore because she had been passed by that first time, when the new Capital was located in a wilderness, came to the front again to put forth an earnest effort to have her way this time. She felt that the breeze that fanned the flame had been blowing good to her door.

A proposed town site of Haywood to be built at the junction of the Cape Fear and the Deep Rivers was spoken of also; and much was said in its favor because the idea was that water was needed for transportation, and such a site would be favorable for a Capital city on that account. This last is a persistent tradition, and not a matter of written record.

Haywood in the House, Judge Henry Seawell in the Senate, made the motion to rebuild the Capitol on the former site in the City of Raleigh, and the great influence and eloquence of Judge Gaston were needed at this momentous session of the Assembly so to sway the wavering minds of the Legislators that they might vote for the retention of the seat of government in Wake County. The bill to rebuild the Capitol at Raleigh and on its old site was finally passed by a safe majority, and carried the appropriation of fifty thousand dollars. The Representatives, thinking of the twenty thousand which sufficed to build the first State House, considered this a generous allowance. They ordered the new building to be as nearly fire-proof as possible, to be built of granite and to have stone floors as well as walls.

The committee to have charge of the building were William Boylan, Duncan Cameron, William S. M'Hoon (State Treasurer), Henry Seawell, and Romulus M. Saunders. This first committee soon resigned and was succeeded by a second entire body composed of S. F. Patterson, Beverly Daniel, Charles Manly, Alfred Jones of White Plains, and Charles L. Hinton. Mr. Nichols was State architect and had had some experience with the stone which could be quarried here at home. A builder from the North was associated with him for a little time, but was later dismissed.

The committee were men of boldness, for they calmly used the whole of the first approation to build the foundation for the new Capitol and then asked for more. Of course

CANOVA'S CONCEPTION OF GEORGE WASHINGTON AS PICTURED IN A RARE SKETCH AFTER THE FAMOUS STATUE. (FROM MRS. JULIA JOHNSTON ANDREWS' SKETCH)

this was exactly what they should have done, but when we reflect how unpopular this action would appear to the habitual parsimony of that day's public opinion, and how well the Legislature understood that unavoidable taxation was all that would be tolerated, we may understand that in doing this they were tempting criticism and doing it consciously.

On July 4th, 1833, the corner stone of the Capitol was laid with Masonic rites, and an account of the procession and of the articles placed in the corner stone may be read in the papers of that date.

Governor Swain was in office at that time, and on that same day was held in the brick hotel, formerly the State Museum, a meeting of representative citizens of North Carolina to debate on ways and means for building a railroad; or two lines, one east and west and one north and south, connecting with the Portsmouth Railroad, and extending to some convenient point on the South Carolina line. Governor Swain presided over the meeting, the first of its kind ever held in North Carolina, and their decision was to petition the Legislature to assist the enterprise by pledging the faith of the State. A subsequent, more widely representative convention suggested the proportion of three-fifths subscribed by stockholders, and two-fifths loaned or invested by the State.

To return to the new Capitol, begun as above, in 1833, and built for the sum as calculated after its completion, of $530,684, requiring seven years to finish. It is, and has been, as fine a building of its kind as is to be found in the United States, and it it has been a lovely and satisfying sight to several generations of North Carolina folk. The stone was all taken from that same quarry at the eastern side of town which had been opened for the foundation of the first State House.

It is a granite, rather brittle, and veined with lines of brown which make its coloring warm instead of too grey. It is somewhat translucent, having the quality, more than any other stone in the State, of reflecting a different color under every changing sky which looks down upon it. When snow is on the ground, in the glow of a winter sunset, it has a lovely bluish cast. In spring, when the baby leaves on the trees around it show pale green, it looks pinkish and pale grey, and

IMPROVEMENTS AND PROGRESS 189

ethereal like a fairy palace. This wonderful stone gave trouble to the builders, however, and sometimes cracked unexpectedly. One of the great pillars of the western facade, has a broken corner in its pedestal, where a piece of the slab faulted when the weight grew heavy upon it, and which was never corrected because of the great expense involved of renewing the whole pillar.

Directing the building was William Nichols. The architect, Ithiel Towne of New York City, came to see the foundation laid out and begun. He left as an architect and draughtsman to to represent him, David Paton, a Scotchman, who did not remain long in North Carolina after he had completed his work. During his stay, however, he married a North Carolina lady, and his wife died and left him with one baby girl. This child was returned to the care of her Southern grandmother, and married here. Through her Mr. Paton has descendants in this State.

Thomas Bragg, father of Governor Bragg, was also in charge of part of the work. It was necessary also to import skilled stonecutters from England and Scotland, for there were none in North Carolina, and accordingly the ancestor of the Stronach family was one of these skilled craftsmen, William Murdoch of Salisbury was another, also a Mr. Puttick, and others who cast in their lot here afterward and became permanent citizens.

On first coming to this climate these foreign folk found the heat and humidity hard to bear and several died of the fevers which were considered quite inevitable in those days. They lie buried in the old City Cemetery. The most of the Scotch masons adapted themselves as that sturdy race does in every part of the world, and worked busily at the rising wall of the Capitol until it stood complete.

There is no use giving dimensions and telling of the source of the architectural details of this building, speculating as to the Greek or Roman temple suggested by this cornice, or the classical building imitated in that facade, for we may see the lovely pile of stone any day, those of us who live in this city and country. It has become for us like the sunshine and the blue sky, too much a part of our daily vision for us to realize the great intrinsic beauty it represents.

It took several sets of commissioners to finally complete the building of the Capitol, and they frequently resigned, and were often replaced during the interval; for it is hinted that the great amount of money which had to be expended more than the first appropriation caused a good deal of criticism. Also not being skilled architects they must stand by what was told them by their contractors; and many difficulties quite unexpected had to be met one by one in the progress of the edifice. Besides this, every one who passed by felt privileged to criticise and spend an opinion, until those in charge could scarcely maintain their calmness. This sort of free advice is one of the rights of a democracy. Kings' houses are not so pitilessly criticised.

The last committee, those who persisted, were but three—William McPheeters, John Beckwith, and Weston Gales, and it is these whose final accounting to the General Assembly is published in the newspapers of the time.

The stone to build the Capitol was hauled to the spot by means of a little street railroad or tramway, called the "Experimental Railroad." This was constructed across from the quarry to the eastern end of New Berne Avenue, and west along that street to the Capitol Square, and the small cars drawn by mules easily handled the blocks of stone. This plan, which seems quite simple and obvious, was considered a wonder and a great innovation at that time. The railroad idea was quite new and as thrilling to the popular imagination as the airplane is now in 1922. The idea of building and operating this little railroad was due to Mrs. Sarah Hawkins Polk, wife of Colonel William Polk, and she put her savings into it, realizing three hundred per cent.

Among the letters of her son, Leonidas, then a cadet at West Point, to his parents, was one which contributed the idea. He went to Boston on a summer leave of absence, and saw there in operation that sort of a tramway bringing in the stone being then used to build Bunker Hill Monument. He took the trouble to write his parents the whole plan in detail, making a careful little sketch to show the proper flange the car wheels should have in order to run safely on the wooden rails. This experimental railroad was such a success that a passenger car was put on, drawn by a safe horse, and people came from far and near to enjoy a new sensation, so that at times the hauling of stone was somewhat impeded. Street cars were thus a very early development in Raleigh, due to the seizing of a new idea by a woman.

Indeed, the good ladies of Raleigh seem to have been more "experimental" than their lords on several occasions, although we are often told that women are the conservative sex. We have told of Miss Betsy Geddy's spirited effort to save the finest thing in the State, the Canova statue of George Washington, at the time the old State House burned. This story is like that of the alabaster box of precious ointment, always to be told in her praise. One of the daughters of Mr. Casso, the innkeeper or hotel man, had married the merchant, John Stewart. She was one of those strong-willed and practical sisters who make the finest ancestors in the world, because they have the common sense and decision to meet a crisis.

She saved her home, although it was given up to be destroyed in the path of that great

First locomotive running into Raleigh in 1840. Also sketch of passenger car generally used at that time. (From a photograph of model and original now in locomotive museum at Perdue University. The locomotive had a 42-inch driving wheel. The car seated twelve persons

fire that swept off the whole east side of Fayetteville Street. This happened shortly after the State House was burned and shows how nearly Raleigh was totally annihilated by recurring conflagrations. They brought gunpowder, and told Mrs. Stewart that her house must be blown up to arrest the fire, which was come almost to that place. She mounted her roof and defied them to blow her up with the doomed house, and when she had thus gained her point she proceeded to save her house, and keep a roof over her head, by hard work and wet bed-quilts. Another time she saved somebody's store from being a total loss by quenching the burning roof with twelve barrels of vinegar, after the wells were all drawn dry. At the festival in honor of the coming of the railroad into Raleigh, she served the banquet to seven hundred people who sat down simultaneously.

Good fire protection was scarcely to be expected in Raleigh, and the business block was crowded together more than was prudent when the town was so small. A tiny fire engine was bought as early as 1802, and another in 1810, although they seem not to have done much good.

Also there were at one time primitive waterworks, water being pumped up from Walnut Creek to a tank and allowed to run down Fayetteville Street by gravity. The wooden pipes soon filled up with sediment, for the water was unfiltered and full of the red mud which is seldom absent from running streams in this section. Drought then reigned as before, except as slaked by well-water.

Hunter's Pond was the cause of much of the fever and chills that made the city sickly, and only after the fever epidemics of the thirties was this pond bought by the city and drained.

Raleigh by this time was becoming aware of her backwardness. Railroading was the topic and the sensation. Internal improvement was in the air. After so long without taking serious interest in the subject, people had suddenly become impatient of the endless miles which separated them from their next town neighbors. Every newspaper told of the rise of real estate values, the increase in the promptness of the mails, and the other joys of those sections where railroads had already begun to be built and operated. "Let us cease to doubt, to hesitate and slumber, let us tear away the poppy from our brows, let us no longer be the Rip Van Winkle among commonwealths," thus runs the editorial comment upon the following bit of news item, dated February 5th, 1833, Petersburg, Virginia.

"It is impossible to convey to those who have not witnessed a similar scene, an adequate conception of the pride and pleasure that beamed from every countenance when the *Engine* was first seen descending the plain, wending her way with sylph-like beauty into the bosom of the town, and, like a conqueror of old, bearing upon her bosom the evidence of the victory of art over the obstructions of nature."

Conventions were held, stock books were opened and the successive Legislatures memorialized, while, after a year or two of such excitement many railroads had been laid out on paper and nowhere else, and the newspapers thought things were wofully slow moving. Yet when we think of the novelty of the undertaking, we cannot say that there was much delay.

The beginning of railroad agitation and the laying of the corner stone of the new Capitol were accomplished the same day, and the railroad, the Raleigh and Gaston, was near enough to completion to be celebrated at the same time as the finishing of the Capitol building.

The same year 1840, which saw the new Capitol complete from foundation to dome, also saw the first train roll into Raleigh from Gaston, near Weldon, and the feelings so well expressed in Petersburg, of victory over space and time, enlivened the hearts of this city, rejuvenated as it was by these two great tasks accomplished.

The Three Days of Raleigh were June tenth, eleventh, and twelfth, 1840, and the town gave itself up to jollification, speechification, illumination and barbecue. Guests from Richmond and from Petersburg, from Wilmington and from other North Carolina towns, were present. Wilmington had also seen her first train pull into the station that same spring, but the western towns were still served by stage-coaches.

The banquet was served in the new freight depot, empty and spacious, and capable of holding the seven hundred guests. A first shipment of cotton for export had been brought into it just the April previous.

IMPROVEMENTS AND PROGRESS 199

There were five tables ninety feet long, and the banqueters toasted in real, sure-enough liquor, The Railroad, The Capitol, Judge Gaston, "The Ladies" several times, and Mrs. Sarah Polk especially, and separately, although they called her a "Distinguished Female." To read of the doings, one would fear that the banqueters might need help when time came to go home after all was over.

That night and the following there were strings of colored lanterns from tree to tree in the Capitol Square, and transparencies, one showing the new Capitol, one the new engine, "The Tornado," and the third, a "lovely scene of nature" entitled "Our Country." There were two balls on successive nights in the Senate Chamber, whose great chandelier held a hundred wax candles; and concerts in the Commons Hall for those who did not dance.

During the day there were trips a few miles out on the railroad, and return, although the rails, or iron strips on which the wheels should run were not yet nailed to the wooden stringers. "The Tornado," as the first engine was named, had but a single driving wheel on each

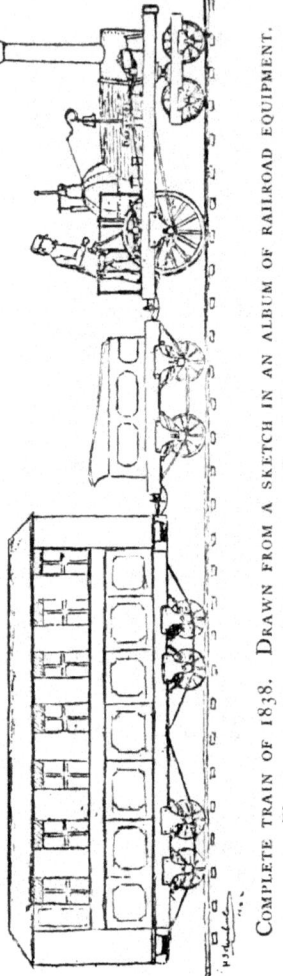

Complete train of 1838. Drawn from a sketch in an album of railroad equipment. The driving wheel of engine is forty-two inches in diameter.

side, and no cab. It was made in Richmond and was similar in pattern to a good many engines turned out about that time. The cars on these first roads were like a string of stages at first, but in South Carolina they had evolved a box-like passenger car, like a low-built street car. Hence we suppose the first North Carolina passenger cars might have been similar to those used near Charleston. All engines had proper names for the first twenty-five years of railroad experience. An item in a Raleigh paper about this time tells of a great railroad spectacle in Baltimore, when the engine came in on the Baltimore and Ohio, drawing seven coaches full of people at once, thirty persons to the coach.

The strips of iron which shod the wooden rails would sometimes become loosened, catch against a car wheel, and turn upwards piercing the car, so that by this means the train would be stopped. They were called snake heads. No one is mentioned as having been impaled by this strip of iron, although there must have been danger of this accident.

The fuel burned on our first railroads, and many years thereafter, was wood. The progress of the trains was uncertain. Sometimes the engine would lurch off the track, and go plowing through the bank a few feet, but it was not a wrecking train and a great derrick that replaced the derailed cars, but simply a couple of dozen men gathered from nearby farms, and a mule or two, for the little engine was not too heavy to be coaxed back upon the track by their combined efforts.

Railroad nomenclature was not settled at this time. They called a collision (and these happened soon) a concussion. A train was called a brigade of cars.

The Raleigh and Gaston was eighty-six miles long, and this distance and return was made in twelve hours, which was considered a giddy pace. The time table given occurs several years later, and says "Leave Raleigh at 7:00 a. m., Reach Weldon at 12 m."

The president of the new road was George W. Mordecai. The State aided in financing the project, although a little reluctantly, and on rather severe terms. We must notice that fares on the different stage lines were reduced immediately, and stages and harness began to be advertised for sale. That the much needed impulse to prosperity was given, farm property increased in value along the new line, and the North Carolina Railroad was soon built, shows that upon the coming of the much needed improvement trade was steadily progressing. For a long time the population of North Carolina had been almost stationary, and from 1830 to 1840 only fourteen thousand five hundred increase was noted over the whole State. Now the "breath of progress and the breeze of prosperity was to blow away all stagnation and sloth."

CHAPTER IX
The Middle Years

I N the decades of the forties and the fifties progress and development of Wake County went steadily forward, even as the prosperity of North Carolina increased. The young men of the Commonwealth did not run away in such numbers to Texas and Missouri as they had formerly done to the near South and West.

The City of Raleigh, established beyond all peradventure as Capital of the State for the future, found herself by central position, and by heritage, confirmed in the social leadership of the State. Her individual social atmosphere began to make itself felt. Then, as at present, there existed a certain indifference to money as an asset socially, a desire to value her new-comers for what they could prove themselves to be, provided that first of all they be agreeable people. This is the quality of a society conservative, and yet liberal; reserved, and yet tending to kindliness and toleration. Such a flavor of life, fine and subtile, does not develop save in a time of quiet improvement, and hopefulness.

In the county as a whole, the change to more prosperous times became evident. There was more to employ the young men of a family and to make their stay at home worth while to them.

Probably most of these plantation homes, with their wide double piazzas and clustering groves of trees, these patriarchal mansions, only a few of which survive conflagration and neglect, were built about 1840.

Some were built later, a few much earlier, but none could have been made after the war. The woodwork and the cornices of these houses were often of a high finish, and the joinery surprises those who think that slaves could attain no fine workmanship. Those were the houses of which the old folk would fondly remark, "I tell you that was a fine old house in its day." These homes seem quite simple and plain, but are well remembered for what they represented to the life of those times. They are roomy, they have a look about them of generosity on the part of their builders, of the spirit of free hospitality untrammeled by the drudgery which lack of servants must bring. They were largely placed in a country not too thickly settled, and provided with the abundance of food and drink which was unstinted at that era of our history. They gave a cheerful welcome and were abodes of gracious leisure. These recollections combine to fill up the kindly memories of these old houses. Indeed the time from the first of the forties through the fifties must have been a golden age to be alive in, the joyous youth of our country.

Improvements in living conditions came in quick succession, and made existence easier, while anticipation of the next surprise kept attention and imagination at a stretch to behold the next wonder that should happen. The over-mechanical development of things which has made our hurry and complication too great was unguessed at that time, and only the delight of growing ease was perceived.

The conquering of space by the railroad, and of time by the telegraph; the increase in wealth and comfort; in the desire for learning and spread of education; the feeling of enlarged opportunity, as the great United States rounded out to its present boundaries; all these elements combined to give everyone a forward-looking cheerful expectation.

The Mexican War, resulting as it did in complete victory, gave the self-confidence of success to our soldiers. The pioneer spirit which in America had so long driven its children further west to find the "Something hid behind the ranges" let only the Pacific Ocean arrest its onward career. Gold was discovered in California, and the mad rush to the West went across the plains in '49. How romantic it all was! Life was a joyous adventure to be met with enthusiasm, to be followed with eager delight.

When reading of the political campaign of 1839-40 in which the Whigs elected Harrison President, it seems a performance boyish and boisterous beyond any that has been carried on before or since. The songs, set to familiar tunes; the log-cabins mounted on wheels and drawn about to represent the home of "Old Tippecanoe" as they called General Harrison; the barrels of hard cider kept continually on tap for his supporters, said to be his favorite drink; the ships in honor of Van Buren (no *especial* drink specified); the slang-whanging by all newspapers; the processioning and the yelling; it all sounds like a prolonged college celebration. The Raleigh Whigs built a log cabin for campaign headquarters, which was twenty-five by forty feet in dimensions. The young Whigs cut the logs in the woods, hauled them in, and built it in one day. Here was the place for the Whig speakings. The Marks Creek Whigs, and others from that side of the county, came in in procession, bringing barrels of hard cider with them. They joined in a whole day's rally, finished up with a big barbecue. The whole State went wild. A log cabin came rolling through the country all the way from Salisbury to Raleigh, with doings every step of the way. It was a merry time, but although all this boisterous party spirit was afoot, yet there were many other things more permanently worth while to be considered.

An interest in education, as mentioned before, had sprung up with renewed prosperity. Almost at the very beginning the far-sighted fathers had established a State University, but there were as yet no public schools as we now have them. These were days of the Academy and the private school. There were many of these all over the State, both for boys and girls, and also we had had a good many more or less successful and permanent in Wake County. Saint Mary's school in Raleigh was at first a boys' school. It was opened in 1834 but was soon changed to what it has remained. Pleasant Grove Academy at Wake Forest was another girls' school of this county. Wake Forest College was founded by the Baptist denomination, and located on the plantation of Dr. Calvin Jones in the year 1833. The first president was that consecrated man, Dr. Waitt.

This was the first denominational college in North Carolina, and has been of untold benefit to the whole State. It was founded under the idea that it should be an industrial school, and this idea was also used at the beginning of Davidson College a few years later. Trinity College also was founded in these next few years, but to Wake Forest belongs the honor of being the first in the field. The industrial idea was soon abandoned.

In the year 1840 was enacted the act which made available the scant school funds of the State which had been accumulating for years, and those counties which were willing to sup-

A PLANTATION HOUSE OF THE LARGER TYPE, OF THE FIRST YEARS OF THE NINETEENTH CENTURY. THIS HOUSE IS QUITE SOLID TODAY

plement their quota of State money could establish free schools. Wake was one of these counties, although not many free schools were opened as yet, and those taught only the most elementary branches of reading and writing and a little arithmetic. Nevertheless, every child of Raleigh should be taught why one of our school buildings is called the "Murphy" and one the "Wiley" school.

Other ideas of reform were abroad in Raleigh. There was begun at that time the first temperance society, and though this died out afterwards, the idea lived on to later fruition.

In the year 1841 the population of Wake County was eighteen thousand, and by the year 1860 it had increased to thirty thousand.

After the railroads were completed, Raleigh might seem to settle to quiet growth because the new era had begun in earnest with the coming of the railroad, and all sorts of new comforts and luxuries hitherto uncommon had come in with transportation. To read the grocers' advertisements, comparing them with a few years before, you may notice how they change from a simple list of heavy groceries and no more, to long columns advertising dainties such as candies, raisins, figs, cordials and syrups, dried fruits, teas and coffees, enough to make the mouth water.

Milliners, too, began to advertise styles straight from Paris, and trimmed bonnets from New York, these last of the coal-scuttle variety, huge and deep, to be worn with dresses which spread and frilled at the bottom like a two-yard-wide morning-glory blossom. The ladies wore tight bodices and large leg-o-mutton sleeves made to stand out by means of cushions at the shoulders.

To match such ladies' dresses, the beaux wore tight blue tailcoats with brass buttons and high velvet collars, nankeen trousers with straps under the foot to hold them down (these were tan colored, lighter than khaki) and high bell-crowned beavers, light colored, and made with wide curly brims. Their cravats were like young tablecloths, winding twice round the neck, holding up the sharp points of their white collars against their ears. Ladies' hoop skirts grew wide or grew narrow according to the fashion, the men's trousers grew more open or narrowed at the foot, year by year, but all through the period I am describing, clothing was exaggerated and extravagant, and many yards of material went to the making of a single costume.

Soon after the coming of the railroad, we see a soda fountain advertised, and soon again, a circus with a menagerie. More amusements were demanded, more luxuries obtainable.

The telegraph was not a common convenience until about 1855, and was not used to run trains by, at first. You did not know what had become of your family after the train had carried them away until at least a week after when they wrote you their adventures. You simply had to sit patiently and wait for the train you expected to take, until it finally rolled in around the curve, to the station.

But indefinite though the schedules were, goods and people could be moved from place to place as never before. A farmer could dispose of his produce to better advantage, could sell his cotton and tobacco at the seaboard. Agriculture, which had become less efficient rather than more so during the first third of the nineteenth century, picked up in interest as its rewards became greater. The articles in the papers treated of good methods, and the first agricultural fair was held in Raleigh in 1833. News items about large crop yields were common, and in 1841 the amount of one hundred ninety bushels of corn to the acre is given as the best record of the two Carolinas.

That other kind of cultivation which is spelled Culture with a big C, and which must be neglected for awhile until a new country has time for it, began in this era to be more sought after. Good books are advertised for sale in each issue of the Raleigh papers. A Richmond gentleman, visiting Raleigh for the railroad celebration, describes his morning spent in the North Carolina book store, and tells of the interesting literature he found there. About this time, sandwiched in among law, religion, text books and almanacs, we find advertised, De Tocqueville's *Travels in America*, Scott's Novels, and Jane Austen's *"Emma"*, besides much other good literature.

The *Southern Literary Messenger* was started in Richmond as early as 1831, and was one of the very first American periodicals devoted to pure literature. On the list of original subscribers which made its publication possible occur the names of several Raleigh people.

After 1843, Edgar Allan Poe, according to many good critics our greatest American poet, was the editor of this magazine, and to it he contributed some of his loveliest lyrics. Books and magazines of the best were plentiful as you see in old Raleigh, and all the means of self-culture were available here which were to be found anywhere in the United States.

But all through these times of expanding horizon and days of dawning culture, there was an undercurrent of discord, a voice of coming storm. It could be heard, so to express it, only when silence fell; like the sound of surf, inland on a still night.

The North and South had been for thirty years like members of a family whose individuals have had a terrible disagreement on fundamentals, but which has decided, for reasons of policy and property, to hold together in outward semblance long after all true fellowship and mutual love have departed. The subjects which divided them, slavery and states rights, were past being discussed as a general theme of common interest.

"Midway Plantation," across Neuse River, a fine example of the plantation home of the middle nineteenth century.

Feeling on both sides had run so high in Congress that full statement of opinion either way was difficult to tolerate. Compromise after compromise had been arranged by first one and then the other party, each side had been soothed in turn; but by the latter years of the decades we are describing, further arrangement of differences in this way had become a stench in the nostrils of either side. One thing only had been accomplished by this continual compromising, namely, time had been given so that the nation had learned more about workable self-government.

Now the time of silent ignoring of the topics which everyone was passionately thinking about in their hearts was nearly past. The calling of things peaceful when all inner conviction was a bitter partizanship had to find a definite end.

North Carolina had been a somewhat backward state, she had been subject to certain conditions which had made her so. Her intense independent individualism had made it hard for her to unite her sons in any cause, and the Union had not been so much a matter of course to her as a lesson to be learned, a course to be thoughtfully adopted.

In Raleigh, as the fifties died, thoughtful men sat and watched all their commonwealth building toward a great Union, crumble day by day. While no one would admit that it was in any danger, all were aware of the fact in their secret hearts, and knew that any moment might set the whole country adrift as in the swift water above Niagara, and that the falls were near.

Young heads might wish a change, might wish to cast the die, to pass the Rubicon; they might tell of what they did not wish to be forced to advocate; but although North Carolina had been late in entering the Union, yet she felt bitterly sorry to leave it.

Meanwhile the young men found the cautious counsels of their elders very slow and cool. Their blood was up. They had no experience of war; but neither had they any doubt of their own valor.

Our good Governor Ellis, truly honest, much tried, and earnestly trying to avert trouble, and those wise heads which stood with him, held back against the current with all their influence, but the young men had got the taste of that exultation which coming storm gives to their leaping pulses. Speech-making might satisfy the elder folk, but they were for launching out. Issues grew ever more tense. Different opinions became always more irreconcilable.

In the spring of 1861, the plot of ground where the Tucker Building now stands on Fayetteville Street was the place where the rival factions rioted. Sumpter had been fired upon, but still there were those who hoped that peace would be restored. Red cockades were mounted by those anxious for secession, and a flag representing that idea was raised, but Union men fired upon it and tore it down. One of the younger Haywoods (Duncan) and Basil Manly, returned the fire of those who would remove it, and as the riot went on Governor Ellis came to quell the excitement. At that very moment, it is said, the telegram was handed him announcing Lincoln's call for troops from North Carolina. Then it was that North Carolina seceded.

Like all calamities, the War of 1861 came suddenly, and was greeted with painful dismay by those who had been fondly hoping against all hope for the preservation of the Union.

Some of the people of this old town were very sorry, some were quite exultant and gay, but all knew where they must stand. The hot secession boys and the men who had hoped and held to the Union all enlisted together; together they drilled and trained, and together they fought, and side by side some of them died, on Tennessee hills, and in Virginia Valleys.

There is nothing that changes the air, that finishes an era, that closes a partition, like a war. Thus ended the times of youthful exuberance, and the tender grace of that vanished day is a fast fading memory to a few old people, survivors of a time which the young must reconstruct to their minds painfully by means of documents and histories.

Many years ago, an old friend of the writer lay dying of a lingering disease. She said to me, then a very young girl, "I shall be glad to go; I have seen so much trouble, I am so tired of life." I wondered at her feeling; I knew her husband, a good man; she had many loving children, and I said so to her. She only looked at me with that pitying expression which the older folk use when some young person philosophizes about the life which is just fairly beginning for them. "Yes, Honey, all that, but you must remember that I lived through the War, and you young folk have no idea what that means."

Those who know by full experience are now very few. It is now that the histories are being written. Careful minds are at work on many a painstaking, earnest book, by which those who came after may reconstruct the long causes and the swift developments of that time of civil conflict.

From Raleigh there went away, with the Boys in Grey, that old, happy, care-free time, and though many good times have come since, that especial "before the war" breezy atmosphere is past and gone.

Reading the newspapers of the time, one is impressed by the lack of hysteria, the clear acceptance of consequences, after the plunge had taken place. When, after the first enthusiasm was over, the grim realities of war were more and more felt, and strong feeling had to be constantly controlled, it was wonderful how cheerfully, to outward seeming, the people could go about their daily tasks.

Before the war was over, heroic exultation had to give place to something distressfully

Costume of a Beau and a Belle of 1810-15.

calm and stoic. Bereavement and economic privation were two things bravely endured, but the painful story of them is almost too sad to recall even today.

When we look over the sea, and remember the things which have been endured, and are still to endure so long after the actual fighting has come to an end and the killing has stopped, we may see plainly how many ills are harder to pass through than sudden death.

A little book, written while the pain of those times was fresh, Mrs. Spencer's *Last Ninety Days of the War,* is a most vivid picture of the mind that suffered in those days. It is a narrative, not a special pleading. To read the book at a sitting is to feel the swell and throb of the personal anxiety, pity and sorrow rise and fall, to sense the privation, suspense, heartbreak and disconsolate apathy, which arise out of too much anguish. It hurts a heart which loves the land and the people too much to be easy reading even so long after all is over.

Perhaps this is the reason that it has been complained of the City of Raleigh, that doing as much as she did do for her soldiers in this last great Armageddon, yet she never could accomplish the feat of cheering her boys as they marched away. We stood stonily and tried to smile, but we never cheered; we knew, for our fathers had told us.

The Capitol has looked on many scenes of joy and grave import. The sky has arched over the tender shadings of its walls for many an April. The young leaves were as fresh and fair in the spring of sixty-five as they were last year. After the last junior recruit had marched away, there came a calm ominous time when the spring sunshine fell on a hushed town. People were uneasy, and stayed at home. Old men and boys were the only ones at home with the women. Streets were deserted, homes neglected, and the stores on Fayetteville Street were closed.

A suspense brooded on the city, for something strange and sinister must be about to happen. Johnston's army had gone west, leaving the city undefended. Over the Fayetteville road they said Sherman was coming. Straining ears of the watching ones listened for the first beat of martial music. Let us quote Governor Swain for the rest:

"It was my lot, on the morning of April 13th, 1865, as a friend and representative of Governor Vance, to find on approaching the south front of the Capitol, the doors and windows closed, and a deeper, more dreadful silence shrouding the city than during the sad catastrophe (the burning of the old State House) to to which I have referred.

"I met at the south front of the Capitol, however, a negro servant who waited on the Executive Department, the only human being who had dared to venture beyond his doors. He delivered me the keys, and assisted me in opening the doors and windows of the Executive Office, and I took my station at the entrance with a safe conduct from General Sherman in my mind, prepared to surrender the Capital at the demand of his approaching forces. At that moment, a band of marauders, stragglers from Wheeler's retiring cavalry, dismounted at the head of Fayetteville Street, and began to sack the stores directly contiguous to, and south of Dr. Haywood's residence.

I apprised them immediately that Sherman's army was just at hand, that any show of resistance might result in the destruction of the city, and urged them to follow their retreating comrades.

"A citizen, the first I had seen beyond his threshold that morning, came up at the moment and added his remonstrances to mine, but all in vain, until I perceived and announced that the head of Kilpatrick's column was in sight. In a moment, every member of the band with the exception of their chivalric leader, was in the saddle, and had his horse spurred to the utmost speed. He drew his bridle rein, halted in the center of the street, and discharged his revolver until his stock of ammunition was expended, in the direction, but not within carrying distance of his foe; when he too fled, but attempted to run the gauntlet in vain. His life was forfeited in a very brief interval.

"The remains of this bold man rest in the cemetery, covered with garlands and bewept by beautiful maidens, little aware how nearly the city may have been on the verge of devastation, and how narrowly the fairest of their number may have escaped insult and death from the rash act of lawless warfare. . . . About three o'clock in the afternoon, in company with

Governor Graham, who had risked life and reputation in behalf of this community to an extent of which those who derived the advantage are little aware, I delivered the keys of the State House to General Sherman at the gubernatorial mansion, then his headquarters, and received his assurance that the Capitol and city should be respected and the rights of property duly regarded."

CHAPTER X

Our Benefactors

AKE COUNTY has owned enough righteous men to have saved many a Sodom. Beginning to count those who have lived their lives worthily before all, the list is a very long one. Singling out from their number those whose gifts have been material, as well as examples in the fine art of living well, we find five citizens whose hearts have been very generous to their fellow men. A society which has brought forth so many hearts bent on service is a society which is fulfilling its best objects, a thing of prime value.

In this summary only those whose benefits were first and especially to the people at large are given. Many donations to causes denominational and causes educational have been made by different ones among us, but we must here notice the more general response to the needs of our city.

Besides these men, there is a woman, and she not a native or resident, who must have her meed of praise for the good work she began here.

John Rex, the tanner, belongs to the very earliest period of Raleigh's existence. He came here from Pennsylvania, about the time of the first sale of lots, a quiet sort of man, simple in his dress and plain in his ways. He is said to have resembled John Quincy Adams remarkably in face. He lived to a good old age here, was never married, and left all his money to found a hospital in the city of Raleigh.

By his will his negroes were freed, and his property allowed to increase until there should be sufficient money to build a hospital large enough for city and county. Besides this he bought a large number of city lots at the second sale in 1814 or '15, which he directed not to be sold until the estate should be settled, and the hospital building provided. He hoped and intended that the value of these would suffice to produce a maintenance fund. The securities which made up the estate proper were much diminished or practically wiped out by the War, and only the lots remained, but Mr. Rex's speculation in these did not fulfil his desire. The part of the city where the smaller, poorer homes were being built extended that way, and this did not permit of the good prices he hoped to realize. The Rex Hospital, therefore, has not equalled the intention of its founder, in that instead of being a well supported institution from the first, it has been struggling constantly for adequate funds. If intentions, however, count for anything, those which gave us the hospital were as broad and as generous and as full of constructive philanthropy as anything which has been done. We have a hospital, and it bears the name of John Rex. His bequest was the nucleus. In 1840, that wonderful year, the committee to administer the Rex estate was duly named, thus beginning another good work, and Judge Battle appropriately enough was made head of the enterprise which was so aided and fostered by his son, Richard Battle, in its later working out.

William Peace, the merchant, left a large bequest toward the education of women, and Peace Institute today bears the name of its founder.

At the time of the War the building was incomplete, and was used in its unfinished state for a military hospital. Since the War it has been an excellent school, maintained by the Presbyterians, and many a fine woman has had her educational opportunities there. Not so old as Saint Mary's, it is somewhat a sister institution, a school, not a college. The funds which were to have made it independent were lost in the war-time depreciation of values. As in the case of Rex Hospital, it is the thought that remains.

A woman's name is associated with the State Hospital for the insane. This stands on a hill to the south-west of Raleigh, which is always spoken of as Dix Hill, although I think the name is a popular, and not a formal tribute, to the good woman who procured the building of the asylum.

Dorothea Dix was a Massachusetts woman, one of those maiden ladies who feel the call to mother the world. Her name stands beside and not at all beneath the names of Florence Nightingale, Clara Barton and Elizabeth Fry. She was mistress of a small independent fortune, and had no ties to hold her in one place, so she could follow her desire of a traveling life in the interest of her chosen cause.

She began investigating the condition of the insane in all parts of the United States, later in Canada, and finally all over Europe.

First it was her custom to make a tour of the State she wished to influence, taking voluminous notes of every poorhouse or prison where insane or paupers were kept. This she did quietly and unobtrusively in the guise of a private person. She made her long journeys alone and fearlessly, and records that she never met with any incivility in her whole work. In the year 1847 she traveled all over North Carolina, and the facts she gathered there she wrote into a memorial to the Legislative Assembly of 1848, presenting it in person, making a stay in Raleigh for the purpose. She was told by those to whom she applied that nothing whatever was to be done. It was pleaded that the people would never permit the necessary taxes to be levied. The Democrats, then in power, had been overcome by such a spasm of economy that they even voted to leave unlighted the lamps which hung in the portico of the Capitol while the Legislature was in session.

The leading Whigs, feeling thus relieved of all responsibility, said that they could do nothing for a new and expensive scheme like the building of an insane asylum with such penurious opponents in the saddle, and so the matter was at a deadlock.

Dorothea Dix always kept a diary of her efforts, and in it she writes of her campaign in North Carolina. "This morning after breakfast several gentlemen called, all Whigs. They talked of the hospital and said the most discouraging things possible. I sent then for several of the leading Democrats. I brought out my memorial, and said, 'Gentlemen, here is the document I have prepared for your Assembly. I desire you, Sir, to present it' (handing it to a Democrat said to be most popular with his party), and 'you gentlemen,' said I to the whole astonished delegation, 'you, I expect to sustain the motion of this gentleman when he makes one to print the same.'" The legislator who took the memorial from the hands of Miss Dix was Mr. Ellis of Rowan, who afterward became the Governor of North Carolina.

The first result was that the bill establishing an asylum for the insane was not passed; but Miss Dix had led many a forlorn hope, and she did not know what the word failure meant. Staying at the same hotel with her were Honorable James Dobbin, afterwards Secretary of the Navy, and his wife. Mrs Dobbin was taken very ill, and Miss Dix, having made friends with her earlier, came and nursed her so tenderly in her illness that when she felt death near, from her dying bed she remembered to ask her husband, as her last request, to champion the cause Miss Dix had at heart. This was the only way she could show her gratitude for the devotion Miss Dix had lavished upon her.

Mr. Dobbin went from his wife's funeral to the Assembly, and plead so eloquently and feelingly, his eyes wet with tears, with such great effect, that the bill passed its final reading with one hundred one "ayes," and only ten "nays." Miss Dix left Raleigh the next December, as she said, "perfectly happy," and the State Hospital for the Insane, which she would not allow to be named for her, is one of twenty established in the United States by her efforts. She was reverenced as a saint, and loved as a benefactress by the whole country, and especially was this true in the South, as it is said.

Dorothea Dix is the only one of our benefactors who did not spend her days among us, but on a subsequent visit she selected the site for the Hospital. She lived to extreme old age, dying in the year 1880.

Stanhope Pullen has not been so long dead but that many of us have known him well by sight, and have greeted him daily in the street. Except as he expressed his opinion in action, his thought was always a sealed book. An excellent but a taciturn man, as to his own affairs.

He was born on a farm near Neuse Station in Wake County in 1832. His mother was Elizabeth Smith, sister of the two Smith brothers, substantial merchants of Raleigh. When his aunt, Mrs Richard Smith, was left a widow she employed Mr. Pullen to manage her estate, and when she died without children she made him her heir. He also managed the estate of his cousin, Mary Smith Morehead, which was left as a bequest to the University of North Carolina. He was a most able business man and everything which passed through his hands seemed to prosper.

After the war, when everything was utterly depleted, and the start toward prosperity

Our monument to the Soldiers of the Confederacy, with the Olivia Raney Library in the background

seemed so difficult, Mr. Pullen used his ready cash in purchasing property in Raleigh, and in this way acquired the Rayner, formerly the Polk property, and he extended Blount Street, by moving the old Polk mansion round to face Blount Street instead of closing it.

Thus was opened the best residence section of Raleigh during the eighties. He dealt most liberally with the city, in giving all the streets, grading and graveling them free. Later he opened a large tract to the North of the town at first popularly called "Pullentown," and sold this off in lots for cheaper homes.

In keeping his own counsel so thoroughly, Mr. Pullen never had it said of him, "Mr. Pullen will do this" or "that." He seldom spoke out his intentions. His mind took knowledge of opportunities, and he made money out of his ventures, but he never gave himself the least uneasiness over the result of his dealings, never bargained or dickered as to the values he set on his property. He offered his land at what he believed to be a fair price, and never apparently cared whether the buyer took the bargain offered or not. That his prices were fair is shown by the immense amount of property which passed through his hands at one time or another. One year he bought quantities of cotton on speculation, and a friend asked him whether the fluctuations of the market did not cause him uneasiness. He replied that he had never lost an hour's sleep over business in his life. He gave to the city the land that is now Pullen Park, and moreover, laid it out, and planted it with the innumerable trees which are there today, growing while he sleeps.

The land adjoining, occupied by the buildings of the North Carolina State College, is also a gift from Mr. Pullen to the State, and when the first building was completed, and the workmen were clearing away the lime barrels and brick-bats preparatory to the opening of the new college, Mr. Pullen appeared with his negro helper, Washington Ligon, and mule and plow, and laid off the drives and paths about the campus with his own hand, and further superintended the planting of the cedars, the magnolias, and the willow oaks which he loved best, and which loved to grow for him.

He personally looked after the repairs on the many homes he rented and all great or small repairs were done as needed, but he refused to be hounded about improvements. It was no use for a good tenant to take the high tone about repair, for he would be quietly and simply told that he might move out at once if conditions were disagreeable to him.

At the same time Mr. Pullen was well-known as the kindest and most liberal of landlords. In his continual rounds, he came to know certainly who was in want, and who was worthy of help. He disliked to be asked for charity, but the loads of wood, the supplies of groceries that came to many a struggling widow, or poor man with sickness in his family, unsolicited and unacknowledged, are known only to the recording angel. Thanks he never permitted.

When Edenton Street Methodist Church was being built, he came and supervised the construction day by day, and saw all go right, but no one dared to ask, "How much are we to depend on you for, in paying for the new church?" After everybody had given all they could, and then stretched it a little further,

Mr. Pullen placed a check in the collection plate which made him the largest contributor to the building fund.

The State College was so beholden to him for its site, that they once sent an ambassador to him to ask for his portrait for their halls. One of the trustees was commissioned, and made an eloquent plea for this reasonable request. Mr. Pullen listened with his quizzical little glance and a lift of his eyebrow, and after the speech was quite finished, he answered very pleasantly, "Well, they'll *never* get it; Good-morning." Hence there is no portrait of Mr. Pullen extant.

Mr. Pullen never married, and lived during the latter years of his life with his niece, Mrs. Lizzie Pullen Belvin, wife of Charles Belvin. He went and came on the street cars, and was always most pleasant to the neighbors riding down town with him; but the next time they passed him on the street he would forget to answer their greeting. Everyone knowing him would say, "That is only Mr. Pullen's way," and greet him gladly the next time he felt free to notice his friends. These manifest oddities only made him more interesting, while no one has ever done more for Raleigh, or allowed less credit to be given to him for his generosity. Pullen Park bears his name, one wonders by what oversight of the giver. He was a great believer in technical training and in the higher education for women. He also gave the site of the State College for Women at Greensboro. He died quite old, on June 25th, 1895.

John T. Pullen was the nephew of Stanhope Pullen, and as a young man was often the almoner of his uncle. Both these men were truly charitable, but while Stanhope Pullen was lonely with the reserve of a man who is independent of others, his nephew was the heart friend of everyone who needed a friend. It was said of him that he served God for a living and ran a bank to pay expenses. The Savings Bank that every child in Raleigh called Uncle John Pullen's Bank, was well and conservatively run, but his real business consisted in his charities, in his furnishing forth of a Christian ideal without a flaw, a life that no one could call insincere or cavil at—that no one could ridicule as narrow, or condemn as fanatic.

Dr. Richard B. Haywood's house on Edenton Street, from a photograph taken in the eighties, showing fence, street lamp, and

Everybody knew and loved him. Children followed him. Men who were not working much at Christianity might criticise others, but they could not say, and never did say, that John Pullen was not a good man.

The poor were his adorers. He was most at home with them because he could do them the most good. If there was a religious meeting in any church he was there; he built and largely maintained a church of his own, which was really of the Baptist denomination, but which was called John Pullen's church as if it was of some especial faith that carried it further than mere denomination could do.

John Pullen's most precious benefits to the place of his birth were spiritual. He was the standard of goodness for Raleigh. True, he gave largely to charities during his life; he gave always and widely to the poor, generously to his church, in many little ways to children whom he always loved; to a tired old colored woman a coin in passing with the request that she ride home on the street car; to a wild and rowdy drummer an inappropriate Bible, which was accepted shamefacedly, and which brought the young man to his knees after many days. He gave himself, every day and all the year. As a young man his sanguine and sympathetic temperament, not yet sanctified, brought him into trouble. He was a bit dissipated, but he left all that early behind, except as the memory of it helped him to speak to the wrong-doer understandingly. Mr. Pullen lived his later life with his niece, Mrs. Kate Belvin Harden, wife of John Harden.

When he died in 1913, the city arose as one man to show how much he was beloved. The factories closed, the school children came, the Governor and state officials as well, together with the rich and poor, while all churches united to honor his memory. The city whistles were silenced for the day he lay in state, and several convicts came out unguarded in their stripes from the Penitentiary, sent by their fellows to lay a cross made of prison blooms on his coffin, and returned to prison sobbing for the loss of their friend. His works do follow him.

Of the five men one remains to be mentioned. The other four were all bachelors. The woman, Miss Dix, although not one of our own people, was assisted in gaining her benevolent desire by a woman friend, so that the State Hospital represents at one and the same time, awakened love for the unfortunate among our people, zeal for humanity in Miss Dix, and the result of a love which blossomed in loss, the fulfilment of the dying request of Mrs. Dobbin to her husband.

Another and the last of our benefactors to this time, was Richard Beverly Raney. He has given the city more wholesome recreation and delight than anyone can know, and doing this has also commemorated an ideal union, a love story more beautiful than fiction. And so the Olivia Raney Library also came out of love and loss.

R. B. Raney was born in Granville County in 1860. He had no chance for a college education, although he was a man who would have profited by one if it had been possible. He had his living to earn. He became clerk at the Yarborough Hotel under Doctor Blacknall's management, being known to the latter as a worthy boy, to whom he gave the position out of friendship.

Mr. Raney made good, was promoted, and finally became owner as well as manager of the

Hotel. He was successful always, and became agent also for the state for one of the best insurance companies.

He married Olivia Cowper, daughter of Pulaski Cowper, and she died after only a year and a half of married life.

Soon after, there was a movement begun to start a city library by general subscription. Mr. Raney heard of it, and modestly claimed the privilege of giving the whole amount and making the gift a memorial to his lost wife. Accordingly the building was placed on one of the very choice sites of Raleigh, facing the Capitol, and was built, equipped, decorated and furnished in every particular by him. After the books, four thousand in number, were catalogued, and everything was in readiness, Mr. Raney had the library incorporated, and conveyed it to a self-perpetuating board of trustees, to be used as a free library for the white people of Raleigh. This gift he made in his prime, and before he became the comparatively wealthy man he was at his death.

During the rest of his years Mr. Raney bought new books constantly for the library, but he refused to dictate, or to take any managing part in its affairs. He would be only one among a number of its trustees.

He married a second time, and the home he built for his second wife stands on the opposite corner of Salisbury and Hillsboro Streets across from the library building. He died in 1909, after his library had been a joy to the town for nine years.

Mr Raney was always very averse to any commendation, and would turn the subject quickly if anyone alluded in his presence to his generosity. He remains a very great benefactor to the city if reform is, as it is said to be, a matter of substitution. What is the great value of an institution which fills the mind with innocent pleasure and leaves no room for evil thoughts? What is it worth to a young mind to reach out and find food and interest which without the gift of books would be lacking? If books are worth what we know them to be worth, how shall we thank the man who made the best literature free to any person who will take it home and read it?

We are beneficiaries of an institution now so much a part of the scheme of things in Raleigh that if it were to be closed for a month, or even for a week, the whole population would be up in arms to reclaim the privilege which they had not sufficiently appreciated because it was so absolutely free.

CHAPTER XI

Distinguished Visitors

ANY people whose names are written large in the books of fame have visited Raleigh in course of its existence. Washington did not come this way in 1791 on his trip through the United States of his day because the city was only as it were, a place on paper. He went to older communities in North Carolina, both in the east and in the west. His itinerary brought him as near as Salem, which was his last stop as he returned into Virginia after his Southern journey.

Lafayette, however, when he returned to America in his old age and went on a tour of the land he had helped to free from oppression, made a memorable visit to Raleigh. He traveled in a carriage with a constantly changing military escort, which accompanied him from one of his stages or stopping places to the next.

He entered Raleigh from Halifax, over the Louisburg road, spent two days, and on the third left the city for Fayetteville. This was early in March of the year 1825. He brought with him as personal companions his son, George Washington Lafayette, and a secretary.

Previous to his entry into Raleigh he spent the night with Allen Rogers, grandfather of Rowan Rogers, beyond Neuse River, on the old Louisburg road, and was met several miles from town by the Wake County Military Company and by the Mecklenberg County Cavalry, come from Charlotte for the purpose, as well as by a good many citizens on horseback, which made a most imposing cavalcade.

Arriving in Raleigh, he was feasted and praised and speechified over, just as Wake County and Raleigh would delight to do in honoring such a national friend. He was entertained at the old Governor's Mansion at the foot of Fayetteville Street. The first State House was then in existence, and beneath its dome stood the famous marble Satue of Washington, which Lafayette contemplated and praised for its likeness to his beloved Commander of the old days. The engraved picture of him so standing with a lady beside him, said to represent Miss Betsy

John Haywood, daughter of the State Treasurer, was made at the time, and a copy of this is still an interesting relic of the Hall of History. It was made from a painting executed by Jacob Marling, a Raleigh artist, who also painted the old State House.

Lafayette, grown old after his stormy life, was a small, spare, quick-moving man, emotional and impulsive in his ways, while our Revolutionary hero, Colonel Polk, was a giant six feet four inches in his stockings. Of course the welcoming of the distinguished guest was due to the surviving Revolutionary officer, who had been his friend and former comrade in arms, and who was at that time perhaps the most distinguished citizen of Raleigh.

So it was Colonel Polk who, walking beside Lafayette, entered the east portico of the State House with him and, pausing, turned with him, so that the people assembled might see the adopted son of the Father of our Country. Lafayette, whose heart was as warm and whose emotions were as ready as they were when he was a gallant boy, suddenly was overcome with feeling, and turned and threw himself upon the breast of his old friend, kissing him on both cheeks with enthusiasm.

A shout of glee rose from the spectators who had never before chanced to see grown men kiss each other, and Colonel Polk, scarlet and embarrassed, his Scotch-Irish reserve all upset, tried to pat back his emotional friend and pull away from his embrace, while at the same time he was unwilling either to hurt his feelings or to jeopardise his own dignity.

Lafayette had forgotten his English very largely, from disuse, and unfortunately had become somewhat deaf. He had a few phrases which did duty for many occasions. He would say, "This is a great country" and "I remember," without saying just what. He would say to an admiring citizen by way of conversation, "Are you married?" If the answer was in the affirmative he would say, "Happy man," if "No" he would rejoin, "Lucky dog."

Now Colonel Polk informed General Lafayette in his first conversation with him of the death of his first wife, whom Lafayette remembered, the wife whom he lost before he came to Raleigh to live. Lafayette did not quite catch his remarks, and as was customary answered, "Lucky Dog!"

To an American of today or yesterday, Lafayette was the sign and symbol of something very precious, of a national romance of history that stirs us to the marrow then and now. His coming was a great honor; his personality was so kindly and so sincere as to fill the heart with warm regard; and when, in a few years after his memorable visit his death occurred and the slow-moving news came into North Carolina, all the State newspapers were put into mourning for him by broad black lines between their columns, customary at that time as showing respect to some great public man or president at his passing.

Lafayette rode out of Raleigh to Fayetteville, whither he was accompanied by the Mecklenburg Cavalry, and was given an especial festival in the town named for him.

Our next great figure who came to visit us was Henry Clay, the great Conciliator, and it was at the time when he was Whig candidate for President. Notwithstanding this he came, not as a partizan, as he announced, but as the guest of the whole State, and as such he showed forth his charming personality. His visit took place in the summer of 1844, and he stayed a week. He made himself agreeable in his inimitable way, and is said to have attended church on Sunday at Edenton Street M. E. Church with the mother of Judge Badger. The story of his Raleigh letter has been told elsewhere. He was by no means alone in his idea that it was not time to admit Texas into the Union, but the minds of the men of North Carolina, without regard to political affiliation, were set on holding their own as regarded taking their slaves at will to any part of the south-west, and neither Clay nor his friends thought for a moment that he would go unpunished politically for the stand he took.

His visit was a continuous ovation; he stayed at the home of Kenneth Rayner, son-in-law of Colonel Polk, who lived in the old Polk mansion. It was under one of the great trees, said to be the white oak which stands in the side yard of what lately was the home of Colonel A. B. Andrews, that the famous letter was written.

A young lady of Granville County presented him while he was in Raleigh with a vest of silk, spun, dyed and woven by her own hand, and made up ready to be worn. This she begged him to wear at his inauguration, the next spring; and he graciously promised to do this should he be elected. But Clay was never inaugurated. He never attained the presidency. James K. Polk, a Democrat from Tennessee, but descended from the North Carolina family, and a cousin of Colonel William Polk, was elected, and President Tyler, wishing to influence history before he left the White House, signed the bill admitting Texas to the Union, action which precipitated the war with Mexico immediately.

President Polk went to the University of North Carolina in 1845 to make the Commencement address and passed through Raleigh at that time, making the first of our President-visitors. Being North Carolina born, he was received as a son of the State, and among his party on the day he went to Chapel Hill was Miss Jane Hawkins of Raleigh, besides many gentlemen. President Buchanan, called the "Sage of Kinderhook," gave an address at Chapel Hill Commencement in 1859. He was entertained by General L. O'B. Branch on his return to Raleigh, and visited Nathaniel Macon before leaving the State.

That great white oak, called the "Henry Clay Tree." It is said to be the tallest oak in Raleigh, as well as the most historic. It stands in the yard formerly belonging to the late Colonel A. B. Andrews

DISTINGUISHED VISITORS 257

We must now tell of one of the grandsons of the County who returned in 1860. It was Joseph Lane, grandson of Jesse Lane, one of the less conspicuous brothers of Joel. He was candidate for Vice-President with Breckenridge, on the Whig ticket that year, and was defeated. Joseph Lane's father, John Lane, was born in Raleigh, but moved early to western North Carolina, where Joseph was born in 1801. As early as 1804 the whole family had moved to Kentucky. By 1822 we find young Joseph already a member of the Indiana Legislature, barely past his majority, and a farmer and trader, having founded his fortune at a time when most boys are still dependent, and in 1845 when the Mexican War was declared he volunteered as a private. He was almost immediately raised from the ranks and soon became a Colonel, and again a few months after he was commissioned Brigadier-General. He was third in command at Buena Vista, and fought at Vera Cruz against Santa Anna. He was the hero of Cerro Gordo, winning that victory against heavy odds. He left the army with the rank of Major-General.

Upon returning to Indiana after the Mexican War, he was appointed Governor of Oregon

Territory, and showed his bravery as an Indian fighter. Thence he went to Congress and was named candidate with Breckenridge in that four-sided campaign which resulted in the election of Lincoln.

Franklin K. Lane, who was in President Wilson's Cabinet, was born in Prince Edward's Island, and was not apparently of any kinship to this man. This last was here during the Great War and spoke before the State Literature and Historical Association, as so many celebrated men have done.

Speaking of the next celebrity who came to Raleigh, we should mention the "Little Giant," Stephen A. Douglas, who had beaten Lincoln in Illinois when elected Senator over him, but whose candidacy was signalized by the celebrated joint debate whereby Lincoln won the ears of the country. Douglas was a wonderful orator and a most eminent man, and was one of the candidates for the presidency in this troubled transition year. Although a Western man there are descendants of his in this State today.

After the war between the States was over, after the assassination of Lincoln had given Andrew Johnson a seat in the Presidential chair, this son of Raleigh came back, not to be feasted and toasted, for in those grim depleted days there was not much festivity afoot, but to fulfil the filial duty of seeing a monument erected over his father's grave.

This monument stands today in the Old City Cemetery, and the visit of President Johnson furnished the occasion for the last of those historical addresses which Governor Swain wrote, and which are mines of information about old times. This is the one in which so many of the less conspicuous folk were characterized, as he gave the scanty annals of Jacob Johnson, the hostler at Casso's tavern, and janitor at the State Bank near by.

Mrs. A. B. Andrews has described her visit in company with her father, William Johnston of Charlotte, to the White House during Johnson's term, when her father removed his political disabilities by taking the necessary oath. She described the man and President, medium in height, broad and stocky, with his neat black dress, formal and somewhat stiff in manners as of someone not too sure of himself. He spoke to her of her name having the same pronunciation as his own, but spelled differently, and asked her from what part of North Carolina she came. When she answered "Charlotte," he said in so many words, "I was born in Raleigh, North Carolina." Johnson's troubles grew more especially out of the kindness he could not but feel for the land of his birth and for his leniency, counted too great, in those bitter times, by his party.

Our next Presidential visitor was Theodore Roosevelt, who came to Raleigh many years later, after Reconstruction, and after many years of wholesome development had gone by and the war of '61 and its troubles had receded into that past time which will heal all things —years after the centennial of the founding of Raleigh had been celebrated, and after the twentieth century was already several years old. He attended the State Fair in 1905, and October 19th of that year found the usual fair-week crowd augmented a good deal by the natural curiosity to see the President, then in his prime, personally and politically, and but just recently elected to the office he held after he had filled out McKinley's unexpired term. He was a man full of virile force, of the true joy of living, and with a hearty word and flash of his famous teeth in a smile to everyone who came to greet him.

North Carolina had given him no electoral vote, but she loved a strong, manly personality, a real man, and so she extended the warmest welcome she was capable of giving. He came in over the Seaboard, and his train stood the night outside the town, near Millbrook, and pulled into the station next morning.

Roosevelt spent the whole day in the city, riding in the procession to the fair-grounds, making his address there, lunching on the grounds, and then leaving town late that afternoon over the Southern Railway. In reading over the reporters' accounts of the sayings of the President on this occasion we are struck by the genial attitude he showed to life. He noticed the children, the horses, the crowds, the stir and the life of the occasion as though he loved it all, and his favorite comment, "Delighted," won the hearts of those who were admitted to his presence.

The plain clothes men, who had charge of his personal safety, had great difficulty in keeping up with the rapid darting way in which he turned in every direction where his vivid interest attracted him.

Roosevelt was here again as private citizen to speak on the subject of the Panama Caanl some years after, and addressed a record-breaking crowd in the Auditorium.

Honorable William Jennings Bryan has been in Raleigh several times, and on at least three occasions was a speaker invited. His oratory was well known to our citizens. Later, one of his daughters made her home here for a time and her noted father was frequently seen on our streets.

In the year 1911, Woodrow Wilson, soon to become Democratic candidate for the Presidency, came to Raleigh after the Commencement at the University where he made a memorable address. He was entertained by the city and given a reception by the Capital Club. He also spoke in Raleigh at that time, and his speech, re-read today, gives a wonderful forecast of his subjects on so many memorable occasions since, recommending so many of the ideas then that he has always advocated since, and advanced as needed reform measures. Its literary form is wonderful. He mentioned on this first occasion the necessity of young men espousing particular causes and reforms, not as connected with or led by some particular person, but as fundamental principles appealing to the eternal sense of justice and righteousness.

The two Vice-Presidents, Sherman with Taft, and Marshall with Wilson, were also here at different times each during his official term. Mr. Sherman, in a letter of appreciation of a reception given in his honor in Raleigh, wrote, "It was a broadening of my viewpoint of our Southern civilization and a warming of the cockles of my heart towards a people that I had not before so well known." Mr. Marshall made one of the most genial, modest and common-sense addresses imaginable, a speech full of kindly toleration, of ready humor, and treating of the pressing questions of the day in that broad and tolerant spirit in which alone they will find solution.

After mentioning our great political and governmental figures well known to history, we must not omit those guests whose values as they came to us were a little different, men who whatever their especial gift, came to us

The "West Rock" at St. Mary's, Raleigh. In this building Mrs. Jefferson Davis and Miss Winnie passed part of the summer of '63, and were here residing while the battle of Gettysburg was taking place

as literary lights, men who were brought here to speak at the meetings of the State Literary and Historical Association.

Edwin Markham, the poet, was one of the earliest of these. The three most distinguished addresses were delivered in the year 1909 by James Bryce, Ambassador from England, 1911 by Henry Cabot Lodge of Massachusetts, and in 1913 by Jules Jusserand, Ambassador from France.

Mr. Bryce is the author of the best book which has ever been written on the workings of the American Constitution. He was one who did everything in his power to cement the friendship of the two great powers of Anglo-Saxon institutions. He was a small, alert man, with dark piercing eyes and a most un-English quickness of movement and apprehension and air of eager interest. His speech was very rapid and perfectly distinct, and was a part of his incisive personality. He was in these days of almost universal clean shaving, quite forested with a bush of white beard, which seemed somehow electric, and to provide him with wireless tentacles connecting with the outer world.

Mr. Bryce has left behind him a charming souvenir of his visit, for at his request, a finely engraved, autographed portrait of King Edward VII of England was presented to the State of North Carolina, and now hangs in the Hall of History. This was an unusual courtesy, for the King seldom gives a portrait of himself, and did so this time in recognition of the antiquity of North Carolina, the oldest of the Thirteen, and thus the first settlement England made in America, her earliest colony.

Henry Cabot Lodge, lost also in a thicket of white beard, but bearing a colder eye, with as intellectual an outlook on the world as Mr. Bryce but with a fine New England conservative attitude toward his subject, gave us a wonderfully written paper on the constitutional development of the United States. This address forms part of a volume which he later printed on kindred subjects.

The French Ambassador, M. Jusserand, also bearded, and with a dark scholarly countenance, a savant as well as a diplomat of a high type, gave from original French sources a delightful account of the friendliness and ideal conduct of the French and American troops in their association during the Revolution. He quoted Count Rochambeau, and officers with him who were present at Yorktown and during all the the glorious episode of that campaign. M. Jusserand was complete master of English as a written medium, but in his reading of his address many were a little confused by the persistence of his accent. William Howard Taft was also one of these speakers, during his ex-president life. His smile and chuckle were in fine working order.

During the Great War, there came to us many French visitors, some, such as M. Stephen Lausanne, sent by the Alliance Francaise, but one party especially, representing the French High Commission, came on a most interesting errand to the Southern States.

The Marquis de Courtevron and the Marquis de Polignac, with their wives, one of whom was an American lady, were making this tour by reason of a hereditary connection. General, the Prince de Polignac of the C. S. Army, was the father of the Marquis de Courtevron and the uncle of the Marquis de Polignac. The older gentleman having been attached to the Southern Armies during the War of

'61, and having thus made bonds of affection which had not been forgotten, his sons were come to renew the association. These gentlemen and ladies were our most charming and memorable French visitors, and the so admirable spirit of war-time France was well represented by them.

General Tyson of the United States Army spoke at the Literary and Historical Association of 1919, giving a first hand account of the glorious history of the breaking of the Hindenburg Line, accomplished by our Thirtieth Division, first and bravest.

Dorothea Dix was a visitor to us more than once in her beneficent journeys, and one is reminded of her in rounding out the list of our guests and our honored speakers.

We must not omit the mention of another woman of real significance, greater than anyone can now determine. That she was a woman, makes the significance all the greater. Dr. Anna Howard Shaw, the champion of equal suffrage for women, the sane wholesome magnetic woman who carried the banner all down the years to assured if not to actual victory, came here and spoke in the Commons

Hall, before the Legislature. She probably represented, in her pioneer capacity, more influence on the coming development of the world than any man of them all. Her sweet reasonableness, her intellectual power, her gift of real oratory, which made men say of her that of all speakers who ever came to us, she was the greatest, all these things should be recorded of her.

She was elderly, rather stout, with a massive face which lighted up into an indescribable inspired look, and a voice when she spoke which, while utterly womanly, had the searching power that filled a hall, and tones and echoes of sweetness that made the hearing an unique experience. It was as though she played on a wonderful musical instrument with rare skill.

A woman fair-time orator was Miss Jeanette Rankin, Representative from Montana, who spoke here during her term of office. She was a phenomenon, rather than an event, but she should be recorded. She was later killed, politically, by the report that she wept as she voted "no" to the Declaration of War, which was a ruse, rather than a true tale. Miss

Rankin was a tall, self-possessed Western woman who spoke well, to the gaping wonderment of many a farmer who did not hold with these "new fangled women-folks."

Long years after the war was over, and years after his summons to the eternal rest, the ashes of Jefferson Davis, President of the Confederacy, were borne in state, from his far Southern interment near Beauvoir, Miss., to a more glorious repose in his former Capital at Richmond, Virginia.

During this solemn progress the remains were halted to lie in state in the different states which had owned his command during that struggle. On 30th May, 1893, the coffin was placed in the Rotunda of our Capitol, there to be visited and venerated by those who loved and remembered him and the cause he represented.

All in this list, and many more, have breathed our air, trod our soil, become part of us for the time they remained with us, and brought to us what they had of value and of information and inspiration to bring.

In other lands, when we are shown a castle or a palace, the distinguished guests, the visiting sovereigns are enumerated, and by having been there they add interest and prestige to the house. So also should it be with a city, and we should count it a glory to have entertained so many visitors who are well known for all sorts of honor and attainment.

CHAPTER XII

These Later Days

HERE is a development and a life story to a nation as well as to an individual, and as the noisy and spacious times of the fifties could only be likened to a young man's exuberant youth, so after the Civil War and its subsequent problems had sobered our people in the sixties and early seventies, and cramped their attention down to the stern practicalities of life, and as further lapse of time confirmed 'this attitude, we may be said to have thus entered on our maturer manhood, speaking always of a nation as if it were an individual.

Young folk are seldom concerned about what has gone before them. It is not until time has ripened their conceptions that they want to study history, look up genealogy, and reconstruct the lives of their forefathers. The very young seldom occupy themselves with old folk's tales. It is so with individuals; it is true of commonwealths; and it has been that way generally in North Carolina. It is a rare and an unusual mind in the past which has really wished to grope backward. When William L. Saunders began the research which produced the Colonial Records on that tiny first appropriation of five hundred dollars, he was still well in advance of the sentiment of his age. Only in the last fifty years have we faintly begun to insist upon building up a true picture of the influences which have wrought changes in our economic habits. For about the same period we have begun to predict the development of the future in a serious mood.

Leafing the pages of "before the war" old periodicals one finds notices of many beginnings of manufacturing in North Carolina, beside the home spinning, weaving and dyeing, and the making of the various articles needed in a simple rural society.

Quilts and spreads were an outlet to the artistry and love of color of women at the South, as everywhere in the United States, in the days when homemade carpets and simple furnishings were the rule. These womanly arts were well exemplified in weaving the coverlids which are made by old patterns brought from overseas, and handed down from mother to daughter. These were very intricate and beautiful, and the yarn was homespun cotton and wool mixed, and home-dyed as well. Usually the wool used in them was colored and the cotton left uncolored, and many of these are treasured today, among the antiques most prized. Homespun cloth for men's clothing was dyed with vegetable dyes in such a manner that the colors never really faded, but only softened into more subdued tints. A wonderful indigo, a good brown, a yellow and a soft grey were among the best colors, while the bright red and the black were brought in if any was used.

Blacksmithing was rough, but the shoemaking was wonderfully fine. This was taught to slaves, as was also expert carpentry, and other building trades. Some of the wooden mouldings that occur, and some of the plaster modeling which centers and edges the cornice of many old houses which have been carefully used, show the taste of the old folk and capabilities of the negroes as well as do their furniture and silverware.

There were wool hats made at some farms in Wake County, and brought in for sale during court week, so that they were called "County Court Hats." This is, of course, a lost art, along with the greater part of the other handicraft and basketry which is revived and treasured nowadays.

Candle moulds and snuffer trays are interesting features of every museum of antiquity, and the sewing, when machines were still unknown, was exquisite.

Cotton was raised in quantity after the invention of the cotton gin, and early the idea suggested itself that it might be manufactured at home without the costly transportation of raw material out, and of manufactured goods back into the States. Many small mills are to be noticed in the forties, and we find stated in journals of the time that there were in North Carolina in that day the quite respectable number of twenty-five cotton factories, employing fifty thousand spindles and consuming fifteen thousand bales of cotton yearly.

None of these factories were in Wake County however. Gins there were, of course, run at first by horse-power, and also the old-fashioned horse-driven cotton presses, which were often flanked with a heap of cotton seed left to rot unused. Not always so, however, in Wake County.

There was over near Rolesville, on Neuse River, quite early in the nineteenth century, one infant industry which was far ahead of its time. Several citizens of Wake County have recently given accounts of a cotton seed oil mill there which pressed ten gallons of oil in a day, and produced much oil-cake, in great cheese shaped masses, as if taken from something like a cider-press. This oil-cake was was fed to milch cows and considered fine to increase their milk, while the oil is vaguely stated to have been "taken to Raleigh." What use it was put to there they did not know. To dilute linseed oil, probably.

A few pianos were made in Raleigh before the war by a man named Whitaker, and were very good ones too, by the standards of the time. The works were imported, and the cases were made and mechanical parts installed and adjusted here. One or two of these instruments are still in existence to show their excellence.

This is not a matter of great importance in the real progress of the city, but is told simply to show that the tide was turning toward the making of things before the coming of the war made necessary the manufacturing of articles for subsistence.

There were formerly two successful paper mills in Wake County. The first one was at Milburnie, and was where a small stream came into the main stream of the Neuse, because clear water is necessary for making paper. This first one was started by Joseph Gales, the editor, for supplying his printing paper, and was burned before the middle of the nineteenth century. The other was owned later at Falls of Neuse, by the father of Dr. W. I. Royster and his brothers, and was dismantled when Sherman's army was near, and the machinery was hidden and saved. It is this massive stone building that is today the major part of the Neuse River Cotton Mill.

The inhabitants of Wake County before the war were, nevertheless a most exclusively agricultural society and did not use very advanced methods. They had felt the lure of the West in those days that swept out the younger, more adventurous men, and the remaining ones were not the eager spirits. Good farmers there were, for as someone has said, there was

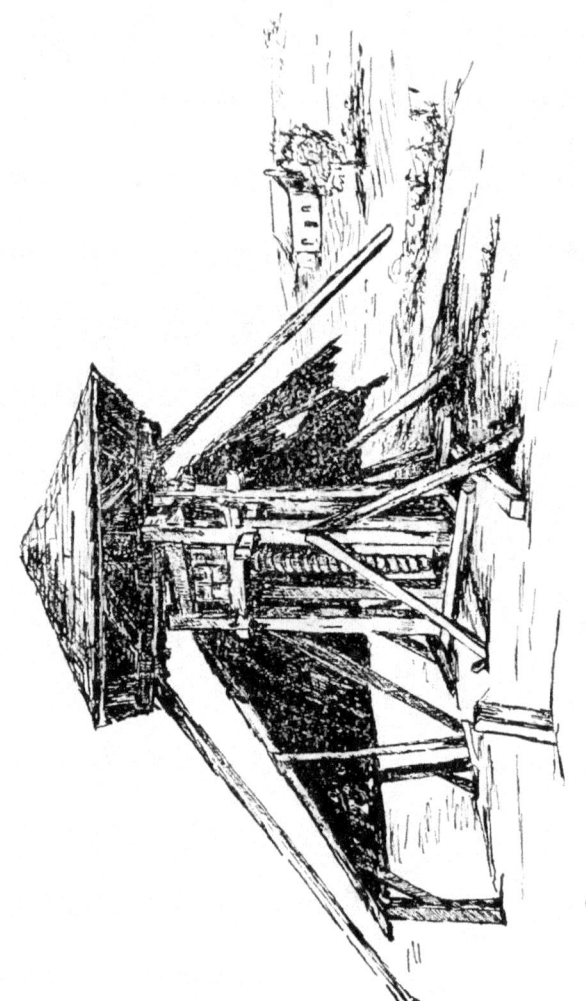

Old cotton press, with part of the shelter still standing. These were driven by mule-power, and were constructed of wood.

no need for a good farmer to move West. But the pristine fertility of virgin land was used up by the customary methods of exhaustion. The new ground was cropped and turned out as old field, to become a prey to gully-washing rains, or grow up in old field pine if circumstances were fortunate. New fields were constantly cleared, and this was the wasteful method all over the American continent at some stage of its development, before the need of conserving fertility was regarded.

The long-leaved pines of the south-eastern portion of the county were soon stripped by turpentine seekers and lumbermen, while the hogs running out kept the young trees from sprouting up. Fear of deep plowing was held as a steadfast belief by farmers who had brought these ideas with them from the sandy country.

We will have to accord to the women a good part of the sudden awakening to possibilities of manufacture which came later in 1861. During the War, the city and county became a real hive of industry. The socks which were knitted for the army by the good women every where were a case in point. Even so late as the World War, when distributions were made of wool for the Red Cross knitting, there were found, all over the country, old ladies who knew exactly what to do with their knitting needles, who rejoiced that they could help in their old age.

After they were taught the "Kitchener Toe," and had been instructed in size of needles, and number of stitches to cast on, they industriously turned out socks by the dozen pair. These old ladies would reminisce, and tell of the sewing they had done for the soldiers in their youth, when cut-out garments were brought to them from Raleigh. Some had made up the cloth for love, and some had been obliged to ask for a little money. All had had their part in the efficient organization of industry at that time.

Powder was made near Raleigh during the War and guncaps were manufactured by Keuster and Smithurst. Cartridges were filled by the children at the blind institution, by the deaf and dumb, and the blind also, who could thus do their bit. Matches and curry combs, wooden saddle trees, and metal findings such as spurs, belt buckles, and other things which could be stamped out, employed the hands of women and boys and some spare negroes. "John Brown Pikes," those unique weapons, were made here also.

Wooden shoes which could be worn by the home folk, and thus saved the much needed leather for the use of the army, were also made in Raleigh and are remembered as having been used by some of the wearers of this clumsy footgear.

When the old Devereux house was pulled down some years since to make way for the development of Glenwood, two bolts of cotton cloth were found under the roof, hidden and forgotten. One of these may be seen in the Hall of History, and while not woven in Raleigh, it was made in the State during the War.

Thus the necessities of the conflict developed the hands and skill of both men and women, and the people who had hitherto subsisted by agriculture alone, found out that if an incentive were given, compelling toward making a start, they were capable of making many needed things, and could become skilled workmen in the doing of it.

The Reconstruction period was a sad and exasperatng interlude, and trailed its discouragement across a land where there was not much beauty or thrift remaining visible to the traveler over country roads, deep in midsummer dust or winter mud; but after the citizens of North Carolina who had the right, resumed the direction of affairs, there was found a good deal to build upon. This was not in material resources, for these were as depleted as it is possible to imagine, but in ideals, and in interest in several things previously carried on with success and efficiency.

The winter of discontent forebodes the promise of spring. Agriculture, as soon as the War was fairly over, made some beginning at improvement, and the high price of cotton induced farmers to raise all they could cultivate. I have been told of a farmer-boy near Raleigh who had by some means raised a fine colt for himself. When Sherman's men appeared they appropriated the animal. As they led it away the boy followed, and duly turned up at headquarters asking payment for his property. He was told that he might have as many of the old broken-down army mules which he was shown in a vacant lot, as he thought his horse was worth. Seeing here an opportunity, he took away a string of twenty of the least disabled ones, and by means of this foresight had mules to cultivate a large crop of cotton that summer, and selling at the high price of the first year after the War he thus made his start.

Mr. Priestley Mangum, a farmer of Wake County, finding that the washing out of gullies and the channelling out of the fields on his farm made so great a loss of surface soil and fertility as to reduce his yield permanently, attained one of those visions of simple expedients which, although they may seem very plain to "hind-sight," have never been thought out before. He found that by throwing up ridges which followed the contour of the hillside, and at the same time maintained a slight but continuous fall of level, he could thus control the water in its course, allowing it to drain away slowly, and sink into the soil on its way. These ridges, arranged at intervals on his hilly fields, obviated washing, conserved moisture, and did not interfere with customary cultivation.

The old Page Mill "down on Crabtree," built and operated by the grandfather of Walter Hines Page

In a hilly country it had long been the custom to run the furrows horizontally around the hill-sides, but a field cultivated after Mr. Mangum's plan had attained the same object more perfectly by its regular terraces made by throwing up a very high ridge beside a deep furrow and then smoothing it into shape with a sort of wooden scraper after the soil was thus heaped up. It was a simple expedient never thought of before.

The first Professor of Agriculture at the "State College," seeing the condition and the necessity, showed how the labor of throwing up these terraces could be lessened by turning several furrows together to form the necessary ridge by means of the plow. So whenever the terraces curl around the hillsides, and the crops grow greener upon the ridges where the soil is stirred deeper and is better drained, we see a real contribution made to economics by a plain man who used his wits to meet his daily problems. This simple plan has been of untold benefit, not only in Wake County where it originated, but also has meant millions to the whole red-clay country of the Piedmont South.

After the first spurt toward improvement, there supervened a long period of depression. Cotton went down in price year by year. The remaining lumber was cut down to the bare soil as never before. Wake County had not made any good beginning at restoration for many years after the War.

In Raleigh there was a certain sum of money which must be regularly spent there because it was the Capital; but as Wake County was neither rich nor level, and as its varieties in soil made it hard to manage, because what succeeded on one farm might not suit on another, a good farmer could just make a living, and a poor one went ever deeper in the mire.

Another time of emigration began, not so much from the elder folk, or from the farms, but from the ranks of bright young men, who could go anywhere where larger rewards were to be found for their labor.

It was during these pinching times that there grew up at Cary, nine miles from Raleigh, one of our most distinguished North Carolinians, one who has not yet fully come into his deserved fame. This was Walter Page, born of a Wake County family, which had been here since early years, one of a number of brothers, all men more than ordinary in ability, and recognized by them as being the ablest of them all.

They agreed to give him the college education which they did not all feel free to take in this struggling time with fortunes to make.

This Walter Page found his mind busy with the problems of the country he loved, where his fathers had lived for generations.

He wondered why it was that men of good minds and good characters, living under a delightful climate, and with no worse soil than was cultivated to advantage in many other places, could exist with so little of hope and encouragement that life was but a servitude to the average farmer. He could see the great need of some change. His first business venture, in the eighties, was the publication of a weekly newspaper in Raleigh. Although this did not turn out a financial success, yet it sowed much seed which has since come to fruition. A circle of young men in Raleigh, himself among them, talked over at length this feeling of futility, this lack of real progress in Wake County and outside. They found a lack of specific information as to real conditions and actual needs of the Southern country, an uncertainty as to the economic questions of southern life, to be one of the great defects of the era. The old formulas did not fit the new times. This coterie, this debating society of young men, not only discussed problems, but decided upon the remedy to suggest.

It is declared by those who watched the signs of the times in these early eighties, that never, until the Watauga Club and the *State Chronicle* put it there, was the phrase "industrial education" ever set up in type in North Carolina.

This Watauga Club, of which Walter Page was one of the leading spirits, decided that there should be an industrial school where boys could receive a thorough vocational training, fitting them for the task of subduing material, whether it be wood, or metal or refractory soil, and making it serve man's needs. They talked the matter over thoroughly, and decided to memorialize the Legislature in behalf of such an institution.

The farmers of the State were prompt to recognize that here was an opportunity.

Under the leadership of Elias Carr, of Edgecombe, afterwards Governor, and of L. L. Polk, the editor of the *Progressive Farmer*, they favored the idea but wished to have it carried further.

They wanted the Land Scrip funds, which came from the Federal Government and which were used in an irrelevant manner by the University, to be added to the endowment already provided by the fertilizer tax.

Private subscription, a State contribution of part of the Camp Mangum tract to the west of town, and the generous donation of sixty acres adjoining to Pullen Park, given by Mr. Stanhope Pullen for a site, were assembled as the assets of the new institution, after its incorporation was enacted. To this the Land Scrip was a substantial addition.

It is an interesting item in connection with the expanded idea of the Watauga Club, that both Wake Forest and Davidson Colleges were first started as industrial schools and as soon were augmented into real colleges.

The first building erected at the Agricultural and Mechanical College, as its official title was first bestowed, was finished by Peniten-

The birthplace of Walter H. Page, at Cary, Wake County, Ambassador at the Court of St. James under President Woodrow Wilson

tiary labor, and the institution was opened in 1890. It was first of all a place where our boys could be taught to win a good livelihood by some creative work.

In the same year was first felt the stirring of the impulse toward a beginning of manufactures, and money was subscribed to build cotton mills, and after that a fertilizer factory. It seems a long time that affairs had been stagnant before the changes began to come, but when once initiated, development has been steady and much has been accomplished. There is as yet no stoppage of this steady development, and it has brought about a wonderful alteration in the look of things. Here and there is a farm run so efficiently as to be really making the best of all conditions, while the whole general practice of farming has improved wonderfully.

The coming of Rural Free Delivery has been a great aid to the farmer who was sufficiently educated to use the help lavished upon him so freely by the Federal and State Departments of Agriculture.

Formerly a farmer had to go to Raleigh once a week, seldom oftener, and would get his mail. It was the exception if he took a paper. Now and then a letter or a patent medicine circular was about all he ever expected. He might hear the news of the day as he stood about the streets, and might return with a feeling of the existence of a world outside, but his wife and children got none of this. Life was stagnant of interest for them. There was now a wholesome change.

Newspapers and magazines became more plentiful, and farmers could read something that was of special interest to their rural life. Now and then a boy would insist on going to the Agricultural College, and contrary to the predictions of the older folk, book farming was found not so unsuccessful after all.

Factories were built in the good old North Carolina fashion of placing them in country surroundings, with rows of comfortable houses, very much more livable, one would think, than the loneliness of the one-horse farms whence their workers were recruited. These factory suburbs, with pleasant gardens to each little home, are seen on several sides of Raleigh.

The spread of the plant of the State College over the hills to the west goes on; a new building or so breaks into the skyline every year as the boys keep coming; while the well cultivated acres of the College Farm extend further, and the big cattle barns are almost at Method. Here we see another outpost of Raleigh.

In the town proper, inside the city limits, the two older schools for girls, Saint Mary's and Peace, with the newer Meredith College (Baptist), bigger and more advanced in standard than either, make the school population of Raleigh amount to thousands of young folk each winter.

The State offices are growing greater each year as the social service side of the government reaches out more and more in influence for good each year. We have had the State Hospital for the Insane, and the institutions for the blind, and for the colored deaf, dumb and blind, for many years. There are two colored schools for higher education, supported by Northern capital, and there is at Method a village of negroes and also an industrial school for the colored race, both founded by the generosity of one of their own people, a man of means.

This city of Raleigh while it is not yet an overgrown, swollen metropolis, is as pretty and as pleasant looking, as busy and hopeful a place today as any city of its size in the United States.

Its people are the same that they ever have been. Newcomers are made welcome to follow our own ways. The homogeneity of society in this city makes for the kindliest feeling between all classes, and it is a town of homes, of moderate fortunes, and of many children.

As you ride out on any of these thirteen great highways that extend in every direction like the spokes of a wheel, you find yourself in a smiling country. One can ride for hundreds of miles over the good roads of Wake County without repeating a single mile.

Of the smaller towns which girdle the County round, there is Cary, birthplace of the Pages, a small town before the War; Apex seven miles further, which was also a small village until the railroads made it a good sized country town; Garner grown up on the Southern Railroad, as Apex on the Seaboard; Zebulon and Wendell, sister towns with their great rural High School buildings standing half way between them, and their streets of pleasant homes, none over twenty years old.

Wake Forest has been a town since 1833, when Wake Forest College began its beneficent career, and now it has beside the college, its own cotton factory, in its own country suburb.

Other places have their factories and schools also. Rolesville has not had a railroad to build her up, and while perhaps the oldest community outside Raleigh, has not increased since the War. Fuquay Springs, where mineral water attracted people for health, has become a good tobacco market, and has grown rapidly since the railroad came, while the water remains as good as ever. They, too, have their school building, as has Holly Springs. In Cary the Rural Life High School dominates the town as is fitting in Walter Page's old home.

With churches and schools and farms and factories, and descendants of those good old families who came here to build our first civilization, and with those like-minded who have come in to help them and continue it, this County of Wake is a most pleasant, wholesome place in which to live.

As one young person who was forced to move away from the old town of Raleigh quite unwillingly was heard to say, "Don't you know that the finest people in the whole world live right here in Raleigh?" And this world is made up of folks far more than it is made up of acres, or of climate or of resources or of dollars.

Given the right folks, a place can be as worth-while as one pleases.

North Carolina Society of the Colonial Dames of America

Wake County Committee

Chairmen
Mrs. Spier Whitaker
Mrs. Elvira Worth Moffitt
Mrs. Alexander Boyd Andrews
Mrs. Franklin McNeill
Mrs. William Johnston Andrews

Secretaries
Mrs. Harry Loeb
Mrs. James J. Thomas
Mrs. Joseph Redington Chamberlain

Assistant Secretary
Miss Martha Hawkins Bailey

Treasurers
Mrs. Harry Loeb
Mrs. J. J. Thomas
Mrs. S. W. Brewer

Custodian of House in which President Andrew Johnson was Born
Mrs. S. W. Brewer

WAKE COUNTY COMMITTEE

Mrs. John Anderson
(Lucy Worth London)

*Mrs. Alexander Boyd Andrews
(Julia Martha Johnston)

*Mrs. Alexander Boyd Andrews, Jr.
(Helen May Sharples)

Mrs. William Johnston Andrews
(Augusta Webb Ford)

§ Mrs. William H. Bagley
(Adelaide Ann Worth)

Miss Martha Hawkins Bailey

Mrs. Thomas Walter Bickett
(Fannie Yarborough)

Mrs. Samuel Waite Brewer
(Bessie Sarissa Felt)

Mrs. Richard S. Busbee
(Margaret Simons Clarkson)

*Mrs. Baldy A. Capehart
(Lucy Catherine Moore)

Mrs. Joseph Redington Chamberlain
(Hope Summerell)

*Mrs. Walter Clark
(Susan Washington Graham)

Mrs. W. A. Graham Clark
(Pearl Chadwick Heck)

Mrs. Collier Cobb
(Mary Knox Gatlin)

---
*Deceased
§ Transferred to other Committees

WAKE COUNTY COMMITTEE

Mrs. J. S. Cobb
  (Jane Williams)
Mrs. James H. Gordon
  (Betsey Louise London)
Mrs. Josephus Daniels
  (Addie Worth Bagley)
Miss Sallie Dortch
Mrs. George Dix
  (Janet Dortch)
Mrs. David I. Fort
  (Elizabeth Robinson)
§Mrs. Leo Foster
  (Mary Marshall Martin)
Miss Caroline Brevard Graham
Mrs. B. H. Griffin
  (Margaret Smith)
Mrs. Hubert Haywood
  (Emily Ryan Benbury)
Mrs. J. M. Heck
  (Mattie A. Callendine)
Mrs. John W. Hinsdale
  (Ellen Devereux)
Miss Mary Hilliard Hinton
*Mrs. Alexander Q. Holladay
  (Virginia Randolph Bolling)
Mrs. Erwin Allan Holt
  (Mary Warren Davis)

---

*Deceased
§ Transferred to other Committees

Mrs. Armistead Jones
(Nannie Branch)

*Mrs. Garland Jones
(Florence Monterey Hill)

§Miss Mary Frances Jones

*Mrs. Paul Hinton Lee
(Ellen S. Tyson)

Miss Margaret Tyson Lee

*Mrs. Augustus M. Lewis
(Sara Matilda Gorham)

Mrs. Harry Loeb
(Bessie Armistead Batchellor)

Mrs. Henry Armand London
(Bettie Louise Jackson)

Mrs. Henry M. London
(Mamie Elliot)

Mrs. Isaac Manning
(Mary Best Jones)

§Mrs William M. Marks
(Jane Hawkins Andrews)

§Mrs. William J. Martin
(Lizzie MacMillan)

§Mrs. Elvira Worth Moffitt
(Elvira E. Worth)

Mrs. Ben W. Moore
(Katherine Badger)

---

*Deceased
§Transferred to other Committees

*Mrs. Montford McGehee
(Sarah Polk Badger)

Mrs. John Allan MacLean
(Eugenia Graham Clark)

Mrs. Franklin McNeill
(Jennie Elliot)

Mrs. James Kemp Plummer
(Lucy Williams Haywood)

Mrs. Edward W. Pou
(Carrie Haughton Ihrie)

Mrs. Ivan Proctor
(Lucy Briggs Marriott)

Mrs. William E. Shipp
(Margaret Busbee)

Mrs. Walter M. Stearns
(Mary Haywood Fowle)

§Mrs. Frank Lincoln Stevens
(Adeline Chapman)

Mrs. Frank Morton Stronach
(Isabel Cameron Hay)

Mrs. George Syme
(Harriet Haywood)

Mrs. James J. Thomas
(Lula Olive Felt)

Mrs. Robert L. Thompson
(Annie Busbee)

---

*Deceased
§Transferred to other Committees

WAKE COUNTY COMMITTEE

*Mrs. Platt D. Walker
(Nettie Reid Covington)

Mrs. William L. Wall
(Annie Cameron Collins)

Mrs. Thurman Cary Wescott
(Daisy Holt Haywood)

*Mrs. Spier Whitaker
(Fannie de Berniere Hooper)

§*Mrs. George Taylor Winston
(Caroline Sophia Taylor)

*Mrs. William Alphonso Withers
(Elizabeth Witherspoon Daniel)

Mrs. Carl A. Woodruff
(Effie Hicks Haywood)

Mrs. Edwin S. Yarborough
(Nellie Elliot)

*Deceased
§Transferred to other Committees

FULLNAME INDEX

ADAMS, John Quincy 229
ANDERSON, John 298 Lucy Worth 298
ANDREWS, A B 111 121 167 254 259 Alexander Boyd 297-298 Alexander Boyd Jr 298 Augusta Webb 298 Helen May 298 Jane Hawkins 300 Julia Martha 298 William Johnston 297-298
ASHE, Gov 93
ATKINS, Rhody 65
AUSTEN, Jane 214
AVERY, Waightstill 183
BADGER, 173 Judge 121 164 171-172 254 Katherine 300 Sarah Polk 301
BAGLEY, Addie Worth 299 Adelaide Ann 298

BAGLEY (cont.) William H 298
BAILEY, Martha Hawkins 297-298
BAINBRIDGE, Capt 106
BANCROFT, 159
BARTON, Clara 231
BATCHELLOR, Bessie Armistead 300
BATTLE, 173 Dr 132-133 Judge 173 230 Kemp 145 173 Richard 173 230
BECKWITH, John 191
BELVIN, Charles 240 Lizzie Pullen 240
BENBURY, Emily Ryan 299
BENNEHAN, R 65
BICKETT, Fannie 298 Thomas Walter 298
BINGHAM, 161
BLACKNALL, Dr 245

BLOODWORTH, 61
    James 75
BLOUNT, 55 61
BOLLING, Virginia
    Randolph 299
BOND, Nancy 99 Southey
    103
BOONE, Daniel 28
BOYLAN, 144-145 147
    William 83 103 131
    143 185
BRAGG, Gov 189
    Thomas 189
BRANCH, L O'B 255
    Nannie 300
BRECKENRIDGE, 257-258
BREWER, Bessie Sarissa
    298 S W 297 Samuel
    Waite 298
BRIGGS, 161
BROWN, Peter 83 127
    145 147-148
BRYAN, Nathaniel 65
    William Jennings 262
BRYCE, 266 James 265
BUCHANAN, President
    255
BURKE, 48 50-51 62
    Edmund 51 Gov 49
    Thomas 47

BUSBEE, Annie 301
    Margaret 301 Margaret
    Simons 298 Richard S
    298
BYRD, Col 25 136
    William 24 26
CABARRUS, Stephen 62
CALDWELL, Joseph 157
CALLENDINE, Mattie A
    299
CAMERON, Duncan 114
    165 173 185 Judge 157
CANNON, Robert 103
CANOVA, 104 106 110-
    111 183 193
CAPEHART, Baldy A
    298 Lucy Catherine
    298
CARR, Elias 289
CARTERET, Lord 72 86
CASSO, 112 160 193
    Margaret 99 143 161
CASWELL, 62 Gov 73
    160
CHAMBERLAIN, Hope
    298 Joseph Redington
    297-298
CHAPMAN, Adeline 301
CHAVIS, John 97-99
CHRISTMAS, William 62

INDEX

CLARK, Eugenia Graham 301 Pearl Chadwick 298 Susan Washington 298 W A Graham 298 Walter 298
CLARKSON, Margaret Simons 298
CLAY, 121 254-255 Henry 120 123 172 253
CLENDENNING, 114
CLOUD, Judge 149
COBB, Collier 298 J S 299 Jane 299 Mary Knox 298
COLLINS, Annie Cameron 302
COMAN, James 103 161
CORNWALLIS, 43 51
COURTEVRON, Marquis De 267
COVINTON, Nettie Reid 302
COWPER, Olivia 246 Pulaski 246
CREECY, Col 93
DANIEL, Beverly 103 185 Elizabeth Witherspoon 302
DANIELS, Addie Worth 299 Josephus 299

DAVIE, William R 62
DAVIS, Jefferson 179 270 Mary Warren 299
DAWSON, 61
DECATUR, Adm 103
DELAIGNY, Maurin 96
DETOCQUEVILLE, 214
DEVEREUX, Ellen 299 John 177 Miss 177
DIEHL, Patricia S 13
DIX, Dorothea 231 233 235 268 George 299 Janet 299 Miss 234 244-245
DOBBIN, James 234 Mrs 245
DORTCH, Janet 299 Sallie 299
DOUGLAS, Stephen A 258
EDWARD VII, King Of England 266
ELLIOT, Jennie 301 Mamie 300 Nellie 302
ELLIS, 233 Gov 218-219
EMOND, Thomas 103
FALSTAFF, John 24
FANNING, 32 David 49 Edmund 31 49
FELT, Bessie Sarissa 298 Lula Olive 301

FORD, Augusta Webb 298
FORT, David I 299 Elizabeth 299
FOSTER, Leo 299 Mary Marshall 299
FOWLE, Mary Haywood 301
FROHOCK, 32 John 31
FRY, Elizabeth 231
GALES, 154 Joseph 103 131-132 145 153 277 Weston 191 Winifred 153
GASTON, Judge 110 124 154 160 165-167 169 184 199
GATLIN, Mary Knox 298
GEDDY, Betsy 142 183 193
GLASGOW, 182
GOODLOE, Robert 65
GOODWIN, Samuel 103
GORDON, Betsey Louise 299 James H 299
GORHAM, Sara Matilda 300
GRAHAM, Caroline Brevard 299 Gov 227 Susan Washington 298

GRANDISON, Charles 133
GRIFFIN, B H 299 Margaret 299
GROVE, Barry 58
GUTHRIE, German 96
HARDEN, John 244 Kate Belvin 244
HARGETT, 61
HARRINGTON, 61
HARRISON, 120 172 Gen 207
HAWKINS, Jane 255 Miss 138
HAY, Isabel Cameron 301
HAYWOOD, 142 171 173 184 Betsy John 251 Daisy Holt 302 Dr 225 Duncan 219 Effie Hicks 302 Eliza 99 Emily Ryan 299 Harriet 301 Henry 170 Hubert 299 John 169 Lucy Williams 301 Miss 111 Nancy 99 Sherwood 103 170 Stephen 170 William H 170 172
HECK, J M 299 Mattie A 299 Pearl Chadwick 298

HENDERSON, Leonard 167 T 143
HILL, 182 Florence Monterey 300 Theophilus Hunter 77
HINES, Thomas 54
HINSDALE, Ellen 299 John W 299
HINTON, Charles L 185 Delilah 74 Grizelle 73 James 54 74 87 148 John 72-73 75-76 81 83 148 John II 75 John III 74 Mary Hilliard 299
HOLLADAY, Alexander Q 299 Virginia Randolph 299
HOLMES, O W 78
HOLT, Erwin Allan 299 Mary Warren 299
HOOPER, Fannie De Berniere 302
HUNTER, Delilah 74 Isaac 57 77 Theophilus 36 40 42 61 65 74-76 Theophilus Jr 77 Theophilus Sr 77
IHRIE, Carrie Haughton 301
IREDELL, 57

IVES, Bishop 173
JACKSON, 119 172 182 Andrew 118 140 143 181 Bettie Louise 300
JAMES, Hinton 74
JEFFERSON, 175 Thomas 41 105
JOHNSON, 260 Andrew 43 95 103 143 258 297 Jacob 103 142 259 President 259 Samuel 54
JOHNSTON, 224 A B 167 Julia Martha 298 William 167 259
JONES, 58 85 Alfred 141 185 Allen 86 Armistead 300 Caldwallader 89 Calvin 90 112 162 209 Evan 89 Fanning 90 Florence Monterey 300 Francis 85 Frank 85-86 Garland 300 John Paul 86 Kimbrough 87 Mary Best 300 Mary Frances 300 Nannie 300 Nathl 54 85 87 89 Nathaniel First 86 Shocco 37 Tignall 86-87 Tingall 86 Wm 103 Willie 54-55 57 61 86-87

JUSSERAND, Jules 265
  M 266-267
KEUSTER, 280
KILPATRICK, 226
KIMBROUGH, Grizelle
  73 John 87
KING, Benjamin 103 160
LACY, Drury 113
LAFAYETTE, 107 110-
  111 249 251-253
  George Washington
  250
LANE, 62 76 89 155 160
  Annie 148 Carolina 85
  Caroline 155 Franklin
  K 258 Isaac 103 Jesse
  78 257 Joel 42-43 46
  54 58 61-62 66 74-75
  78-79 81-83 85 89 94
  145 147-148 155 257
  Joel Hinton 89 John 89
  257 Joseph 78 257
  Margaret 148 Ralph 82
  Sarah 89
LAUSANNE, M Stephen
  267
LAWSON, 18 20
LEE, Ellen S 300
  Margaret Tyson 300
  Paul Hinton 300
LENOIR, William 62

LEWIS, Augustus M 300
  Sara Matilda 300
LIGON, Washington 238
LINCOLN, 143 219 258
  Abraham 155
LOCKE, John 22
LODGE, Henry Cabot
  265-266
LOEB, Bessie Armistead
  300 Harry 297 300
LONDON, Betsey Louise
  299 Bettie Louise 300
  Henry Armand 300
  Henry M 300 Lucy
  Worth 298 Mamie 300
M'HOON, William S 185
MACLEAN, Eugenia
  Graham 301 John Allan
  301
MACMILLAN, Lizzie
  300
MACON, John 65
  Nathaniel 65 148 255
  Sen 105
MANGUM, 285 Priestly
  283
MANLY, Basil 219
  Charles 185
MANNING, Isaac 300
  Mary Best 300
MARKHAM, Edwin 265

INDEX

MARKS, Jane Hawkins 300 William M 300
MARLING, Jacob 251
MARRIOTT, Lucy Briggs 301
MARSHALL, 263 John 163 Justice 164
MARTIN, Alexander 51 63 James 61 Lizzie 300 Mary Marshall 299 William J 300
MCDOWELL, 61
MCGEHEE, Montford 301 Sarah Polk 301
MCKEE, James 160
MCKEITHAN, Dugald 160
MCKETHAN, Martha 99
MCKINLEY, 260
MCNEILL, Franklin 297 301 Jennie 301
MCPHEETERS, Dr 114 151 153 171 174 William 96 113 170 191
MEARES, John 160
MEARS, Winifred 99
MILLER, Gov 105
MOFFITT, Elvira Worth 297 300
MOORE, 62 Ben W 300

MOORE (cont.) Katherine 300 Lucy Catherine 298
MORDECAI, 95 George 174 George W 202 Moses 148
MOREHEAD, Mary 161 Mary Smith 235
MOSELY, Edward 26
MURDOCH, William 190
MURRAY, James 127
NASH, 62 112 Frank 33 Judge 157
NEWMAN, 173
NICHOLS, 109 185 John 106 William 106 189
NIGHTINGALE, Florence 231
O'BRIEN, Ann 99
PADDISON, Hannah 99
PAGE, 294 A F 161 Sheriff 161 Walter 286-288 295
PAINE, Tom 175
PARISH, Susannah 99
PATON, David 189
PATTERSON, S F 185
PEACE, 153 Joseph 103 William 143 153 172 230
PECK, 149-150

PECK (cont.)
  William 103 148
PERSON, 61
PILLEN, 237
PLUMMER, James Kemp 301 Lucy Williams 301
POE, Edgar Allen 215
POLIGNAC, Marquis De 267 Prince De 267
POLK, Bishop 178-179
  Col 112 139-143 177 182 251-252 254
  James K 255 L L 289
  Leonidas 142 163 173-174 177 192 Leonidas K 107 138-139 Lonnie 151 President 107 138 255 Sarah 99 199
  Sarah Hawkins 192
  William 107 138 163 174 192 255
POTTER, 112 Henry 103 S W 99
POU, Edward W 301
PRIESTLY, Dr 132
PROCTOR, Ivan 301
  Lucy Briggs 301
PULLEN, 238-240 244
  John 243 John T 241
  Stanhope 235 241 289
PUTTICK, 190

RABOTEAU, John 103
  John S 161
RALEIGH, Walter 63
RANEY, 247 Olivia 246
  Richard Beverly 245
RANKIN, 270 Jeanette 269
RAYNER, Kenneth 165 254
REX, John 161 229-230
ROBINSON, Eliz 299
ROCHAMBEAU, Count 267
ROGER, Michael 42
ROGERS, Allen 250
  Rowan 250 Willis 103
ROOSEVELT, 261-262
  Theodore 260
ROYSTER, David 161 W I 277
RUSSELL, Earl Of Bedford 41
RUTHERFORD, 55
SAUNDERS, Brittain 54
  Romulus M 185
  William L 273
SCOTT, 214 William 103
SEAWELL, Henry 75 156 184-185 Judge 148
SHARPLES, Helen May 298

SHAW, Anna Howard 268
   Priscilla 99
SHERMAN, 224 263 277
   282 Gen 225 227
SHIPP, Margaret 301
   William E 301
SMITH, 161 E H P 99
   Elizabeth 235 Margaret 299 Mary 161 Richard 235
SMITHURST, 280
SOLOMON, 136
SPENCER, Mrs 223
   Thomas 105
STEARNS, Mary Haywood 301 Walter M 301
STEELE, 55
STEVENS, Adeline 301
   Frank Lincoln 301
STEWART, John 161 193 Margaret 161 Mrs 195
STRONACH, 190 Frank Morton 301 Isabel Cameron 301
SUMMERELL, Hope 298
SWAIN, 155 Caroline 155 David L 85 154 David Lowrie 155 Eleanor 160 Gov 81 102 143-144 156-157 159-160
SWAIN (cont.) 163 167 171 174 181 187 224 259
SYME, George 301
   Harriet 301
TAFT, 263 William Howard 267
TAYLOR, Caroline Sophia 302 Chief Justice 154 165
THACKERAY, 41
THOMAS, James J 297 301 Lula Olive 301
THOMPSON, Annie 301 Robert L 301
THORVALDSEN, 106
TOWNE, Ithiel 189
TRYON, 28-29 31-32 35-36 40-42 44-45 Gov 73 75 Lady 45 William 27
TUCKER, R S 151 Ruffin 151 161
TURNER, Rev Mr 112 Sen 105
TWAIN, Mark 130
TYLER, 120 172 President 255
TYSON, Ellen S 300 Gen 268
VAN, Buren 120 207
VANCE, Gov 225

VASS, Vincent 47
VOLTAIRE, 175
WAITT, Dr 209
WAKE, Esther 37 45
   Margaret 36
WALKER, Nettie Reid
   302 Platt D 302
WALL, Annie Cameron
   302 William L 302
WASHINGTON, 106-107
   109 138 183 249-250
   Gen 43 George 104-
   105 193
WESCOTT, Daisy Holt
   302 Thurman Cary 302
WHEELER, 225
WHITAKER, 276 Fannie
   De Berniere 302 Spier
   297 302
WHITE, Anna 99 Eleanor
   160 John 82 William
   160

WHITNEY, 68 144
WIATT, Capt 161-162
WILLIAMS, Eliza 99 Jane
   299 Rebecca 99
WILSON, 263 President
   258 Woodrow 262
WINSTON, Caroline
   Sophia 302 George
   Taylor 302
WITHERS, Eliazabeth
   Witherspoon 302
   William Alphonso 302
WOODRUFF, Carl A 302
   Effie Hicks 302
WORTH, Adelaide Ann
   298 Elvira E 300
WYATT, Capt 160 John
   103
YANCEY, Bartlett 123
YARBOROUGH, Edwin
   S 302 Fannie 298
   Nellie 302

www.ingramcontent.com/pod-product-compliance
Lightning Source LLC
Chambersburg PA
CBHW071957220426
43662CB00009B/1170